More Advance Praise for *Woke Jesus*

This book should be on the desk of every Christian leader, because we can't keep ignoring the threat, and this information is a road map for the way out.

> —Phil Cooke, PhD, Author of *The Way Back: How Christians Blew Our Credibility and How We Get It Back*

Miles understands the dangerous Woke trend and has been bravely leading the fight against Progressive ideology within the church. I believe in his work and pray that believers everywhere give ear to his message.

> —Dr. Jim Garlow, Founder and CEO, Well Versed

Woke Jesus is an essential read!

> —Kevin McGary, Founder, Every Black Life Matters (EBLM)

The resource every Christian needs, not only in their library but also in their heart.

> —David and Jason Benham, Bestselling Authors

A masterful job weaving church history with Biblical theology in a clear and practical way that will open your eyes to encounter and embrace Jesus Christ that is consistent with scripture.

> —Jason Jimenez, Founder and President of Stand Strong Ministries and Author of *Challenging Conversations: A Practical Guide to Discuss Controversial Topics in the Church*

Every conservative, Christian, Catholic, and Jewish thought leader in this nation needs this book!
—Dave Dias, Chairman, Foundations of Freedom

Wow! This one is an eye-opener. Extremely well-researched and powerful!
—Edgar Struble, Producer, *The Heart Mender* and Music Director and *The Academy of Country Music Awards*

However well-intended, Wokeism actually creates the very injustices it's supposed to end, hurting the most vulnerable people while dividing church and country. Lucas Miles exposes this and provides a liberating, Christ-centered way forward."
—Dr. Frank Turek, Coauthor of *I Don't Have Enough Faith to Be an Atheist* and President CrossExamined.org

Scripture presents Jesus as the Son of God who is truth incarnate. In the last few decades, though, Jesus has undergone a "makeover" at the hands of racialist theorists, Marxist political thinkers, and modern-day Gnostics. Christian filmmaker and pastor Lucas Miles calls their bluff.
—Jeff Myers, PhD, President, Summit Ministries

Bad ideas die unless empowered by dark money. Lucas Miles brilliantly explains both. Read this book, a golden key and an arsenal of truth and light. Then, enter the war for the church and nations. For God's glory.
—Kelly Monroe Kullberg, Author, *Finding God at Harvard*, and Founder, Veritas Forum

It's vital that Christians—especially those affected by the powerless Woke Church—read this book!
—Anna Khait, Evangelist

From CRT and Wokeism to the destructive injustice of the "moral" Left, Lucas's latest work is an intellectual smack down of the cancerous philosophies and heresies that have infiltrated every sector of American culture.

—Rick Green, America's Constitution Coach
and Founder of Patriot Academy

If the subject of being Woke is confusing to you, take heart; you're not alone. *Woke Jesus* will wake you up to what's going on like no other book.

—Lance Wallnau, CEO, Lance Learning Group

WOKE
JESUS

WOKE JESUS

The False Messiah Destroying Christianity

LUCAS MILES

Humanix Books
www.humanixbooks.com

For my Woke brothers and sisters—

it's not too late to come home.

Contents

A Note from the Author

Upon completing my previous book, *The Christian Left*, I knew the subject matter was timely, but it wasn't until I began my speaking tour for the book that I realized how extensively intertwined were the deceptions of Progressive Christianity with the American church. As I visited with pastors, church leaders, and concerned parishioners across the country, I quickly realized that while *The Christian Left* offered both a glimpse at the rise of Progressive Christianity, as well as the means to help people recognize the deception of Leftism within the church, more background was still needed to fully demolish the sole foundation upon which the heresies of the Left were built, that is, a false presentation of Jesus himself. To combat this, it became evident that another work was necessary to refute this false Christ and to equip believers to do the same. Thus, *Woke Jesus* was born.

My goal from the outset, in writing this new work was to assemble a definitive resource on the history of Wokeness and its dangerous repercussions within the church (and what we can do about it). In order to do so, it required beginning with a significant historical survey, starting in the 1700s and working my way forward to the modern era, concluding with a revelatory look at the true biblical Christ who wields the scales of justice and calls the church to repent from Woke idolatry.

Of course, as an author, it would be my preference that my readers would be able to consume every word in the order in which they were intended, but I know that many in our nation are facing immediate threat from Woke culture and might require a quicker path to the solutions contained within this book than a more thorough leisurely reading might allow. If this is the position you find yourself in, please receive my permission as the author from the beginning to modify your course through *Woke Jesus*.

With that said, I've intentionally provided two ways to read the book. For the best reading, I recommend starting at the beginning as to not miss out on the history of the heretical antecedents of Wokeness contained within the first three chapters. For those who desire to jump straight into the modern implications of Wokeism, a secondary option would be to start with Chapter 4, *Critical Race Theory*, and work your way to the end of the book before eventually circling back to the first three chapters in order to round out your understanding of the material.

Most important, whatever path you choose, I pray that this book will empower you to overcome the ideological corruption that is facing the church (as well as our nation at large) and grant you the tools, both spiritually and practically, to "take captive every thought to make it obedient to Christ."

Sincerely,

Lucas Miles

Introduction

By means of specious and plausible words, they cunningly
allure the simple-minded to inquire into their system; but
they nevertheless clumsily destroy them, while they initi-
ate them into their blasphemous and impious opinions . . .
and these simple ones are unable, even in such a matter, to
distinguish falsehood from truth.

IRENAEUS OF LYONS

Irenaeus, a second-century church father, penned these words
while addressing the reason why the first-century church struggled
to clearly refute Gnosticism. The Bishop of Lyon, known best for
his work *Against Heresies*, revealed that it was the complexities of
Gnosticism that made it difficult for the first Christians to dismantle—so much so, that the heretics often easily lured undisciplined
Christians over to their cause. Like two tangled fishing lines, the
early church was charged with the task of painstakingly unravel-
ing the heretical beliefs of the Gnostics, whom Irenaeus called "evil
interpreters of the good word of revelation,"[1] in order to salvage the

true doctrine of the church and rescue those who were ensnared by their deceptions.

Likewise, the twenty-first-century church is faced with an uncannily similar challenge to sort through a neo-Gnostic ideology, rooted in Hegelian and Marxist thought, reinforced by nefariously crafted arguments from feminists, diversity officers, Critical Theorists, communist elites, social justice activists, and "Woke" pastors. It's a massively woven and deeply confusing tapestry of lies that few have properly dismantled well enough for the rest of us to comprehend the full extent of their error.

Coming before me in this work are brilliant thinkers, both past and present,[2] who have answered the call to defend the faith from a strange Gospel. My hope is to build upon their work, while adding to the conversation unique ideas designed to untangle our lines and draw people back to foundational Christian truths. I fear that if we don't do so soon, we risk there not being enough Christians left in America to properly defend the theological walls of the faith.

To demonstrate how far we've truly fallen, a national survey by Gallup found that only 24 percent of Americans now believe that scripture is "the actual word of God, and is to be taken literally, word for word,"[3] a record low based on 40 years of polling research. Perhaps even more concerning is the largest subset of Christians who, according to the same poll, believe the Bible is "inspired by God, but shouldn't all be taken literally."[4] While this may sound like a win, this downgraded view of the Bible reveals how Progressive Christianity has gained such a strong foothold over the last decade.

While a non-literal view of a seven-day creation or whether Jonah was really swallowed by a whale may not seem like a great threat to orthodoxy, this diminished view of scripture exposes the real cancer—a distrust in God. Reminiscent of Eden, the question looming within the ethos of the Postmodern church, and arguably all of humanity, is: "Did God really say . . . ?"[5] Beginning with this seed of doubt, scriptures are scrutinized, doctrines are dismantled, and moral boundaries are moved until what remains can hardly be called "Christian."

The resulting distilled faith goes by many names, including "the Christian Left," "Progressive Christianity," or "Woke Christianity." It abandons traditional biblical interpretations regarding marriage, gender, racial equality, justice, original sin, heaven and hell and salvation, and replaces them within a new fabricated morality, built around political correctness, cancel culture, hedonistic values, obsession with public health, allegiance to the Leftist state, universalism, and virtue signaling. Within its ranks are powerful foot soldiers, many of whom were once reliable pillars of the faith, but who have since deserted evangelicalism or have "de-converted" from the faith in one form or another.

In this sense, John's warning to the first-century church feels all too familiar: "They went out from us, but they did not really belong to us. For if they had belonged to us, they would have remained with us; but their going showed that none of them belonged to us."[6]

Multiple factors have likely contributed to this recent exodus from biblical Christianity, including a rise in progressivism within culture, an overreaction to narrow-minded fundamentalism, the impact of isolation during government-mandated shutdowns for COVID-19, as well as the liberal takeover of Christian higher education. But more inherent in the systemic shift of the church toward Wokeness is the gradual evolution of thought among Christians, both the theologically trained and the laity alike, to elevate Jesus's humanity over His divinity, laying the groundwork for a widely accepted social Gospel.

This tension in Christology, between human and divine, is hardly foreign to Christian history and has been dealt with abundantly by diverse Christian minds, such as Anselm, Athanasius, and Augustine. Despite their efforts, a novel view of Christ has emerged and overemphasizes the humanity of the carpenter's son, known as the "Historical Jesus," which transforms the Lamb of God from the

Savior of the World to a great moral example and a champion of the State. The genesis of this shift inevitably can be traced back to Immanuel Kant, the influential eighteenth-century German philosopher, who taught that Christ was "totally human"[7] and "the prototype of a humanity well-pleasing to God."[8]

Stephen R. Palmquist reminds us that, "For anyone with a theology grounded on Jesus's divinity, this is a roadblock" as "Kant's philosophy leaves no room for a savior."[9] Kant feared that if Jesus was in fact heavenly, He would be of "no benefit to us"[10] as an earthly example because humanity would be unable to emulate His righteousness, devoid of a divine nature. Completely misinterpreting the message of the cross,[11] if salvation was to be found, according to Kant, it was rooted in morality and a pure disposition and not a Savior from Heaven.

With such a humanistic interpretation, it's hardly a stretch to say that Kant was a progressive at heart, but his philosophy was somewhat safeguarded by a dominant Christian moral that lingered from the Protestant Reformation. So while Kant spoke of Jesus, the value of the scriptures, and the importance of religion, his religion was "the pure religion of reason"[12] and not the Christian faith. Supporters of Kant's "morally-focused interpretations of a variety of Christian doctrines"[13] would then claim his criticism of the Christian faith and that of Christ were intended to create "a more religiously authentic foundation for religion,"[14] Kant's version of Christianity. But much like progressives today, this falls incredibly short of encapsulating even basic Gospel truths, such as grace, forgiveness, and the gift of righteousness. What it *did* do was firm up a new critical way to read the scriptures and to evaluate the man from Galilee.

And while our look into the origins of the Woke Jesus being touted by the Left doesn't end with Kant, he does mark the beginning of a spiritual viewpoint upheld by Progressive Christians today, that reduces Christ to a mere revolutionary, prophet, or sage.[15] Much like Kant, whether or not these individuals actually believe that Jesus is the Christ seems to be of little use as "rational human beings . . .

never allow this belief to intervene in practical matters."[16] Because of this, for today's Christian Left, Jesus is only useful to the degree that His behavior aligns with liberal "morals" that support a progressive view of race, gender, and sexuality.

In order to accomplish this, this form of Jesus will need to bow at the feet of Marx, kneel in solidarity with Black Lives Matter, and feel oppressed and alienated by His olive-colored Middle Eastern skin. This Jesus must reject meritocracy and be sensitive to micro-aggressions, conscious of intersectionality, double masked, triple vaxxed, and, of course, sexually nonbinary. This Jesus will need to be Woke.

CHAPTER 1

Jesus the Luminous

Reimagining the Church

"The timeline of the Holy Spirit is driving our decision to launch the LMX at this moment and we are following her call,"[1] reasoned Reverend Althea Spencer-Miller, a leader in the recently formed Liberation Methodist Connexion (LMX).

Spencer-Miller isn't shy about revealing the new socially and theologically progressive Methodist denomination's goal, which is to "reimage what it means to follow Jesus,"[2] and has started by reimagining God using the female pronouns "she/her." Other denominational leaders promise "no doctrinal litmus tests"[3] for those wishing to affiliate with the LMX as they seek to dismantle the "powers, principalities and privileges"[4] associated with "White normativity" in the church.

The demolition of White hetero-normativity, a belief that church doctrine is controlled by a White Eurocentric male theological hegemony, is a major objective for most theologically progressive denominations. As such, groups like the LMX claim to be "justice oriented"[5] as they strive to right the church's wrongs. These perceived wrongs include: colonialism, White supremacy, economic injustices, patriarchy, sexism, clericalism, ableism, ageism, trans-phobia, and heteronormativity.[6]

This collective pursuit among the Christian Left has given birth to Woke Christianity.

Woke Christianity, also known as "Conscious Christianity," is broad-stroke terminology describing Christians who are inten-tionally conscious of oppression, racism, and injustice. Author and pastor Eric Mason says the term implies "being socially aware of issues that have systemic impact."[7] Often compared to the wise virgins in Matthew 25, Woke individuals strive to stay "awake" to issues of social justice while waiting for the Bridegroom to return. Consequently, the term "Woke Christians" describes believers who subscribe, whether knowingly or unknowingly, to the alternative Gospels of Critical Theory, including Critical Race Theory (CRT) and its pseudo-Christian counterpart, Liberation Theology.

Like all heresy, Woke Christianity is rooted in an element of truth (as in God's opposition to injustice), but it encapsulates this truth with a convincing web of anti-biblical ideology and extremism. As such, scripture is either downgraded, stripped of its authority, or frequently ignored, as personal experience, like suffering or oppression, and per-sonal enlightenment take center stage in crafting Woke theology.

For those new to such terminology, Critical Theory has evolved from a highly academic and abstract ideology (developed as early as 1923 in the Institute for Social Research in Frankfurt, Germany)[8] to a mainstream worldview that is shaping sermons, public policy,[9] grade-school curriculum,[10] and even medical advice.[11]

It is "chiefly concerned with revealing hidden biases," especially those related to race, gender, and socioeconomics. Due to perceived systemic problems inherent within existing social systems, Critical Theorists advocate for dismantling and deconstructing the current systems (such as capitalism, religion, or even America) rather than working within the system to generate improvement.

Liberation Theology (like its cousin Black Liberation Theology) is a type of religiously motivated Critical Theory that "depends upon the Marxist system"[12] to dismantle perceived injustices in oppressed people groups, even if that requires revolt and revolution.[13]

Both Critical Theory and Liberation Theology, doctrines that few took seriously, are creating a schism, and if allowed to grow, may arguably rival the doctrinal differences of the Protestant Reformation. In fact, Critical Theory was a major topic of conversation as the Southern Baptist Convention (SBC) voted in a new president, Ed Litton, in summer 2021. Litton was viewed by many as a "Woke"[14] theologian after apologizing for former views on both systemic racism and homosexuality, marking a major step backward in establishing a top-down biblical orthodoxy within the SBC. Litton joins the ranks of other SBC influencers (e.g., Russell Moore, J. D. Greear, and former SBC member Beth Moore)[15] who have backpedaled on scriptural truths and used their platforms to facilitate Woke doctrines.

The Evolution of Critical Theory

While many may be acquainted with the dangers of Critical Theory (e.g., restriction of free thought, perpetuation of victimhood, indoctrination of young people, a distorted moral fabric, and undue resentment toward the Western world), few seem to fully grasp the ideological and religious scaffolding that not only shaped but still guides Critical Theorists, from pedagogues to protesters.

While conservative parents and pundits actively attempt to refute and dismantle the collective dogmas of Wokeism, Critical Theory, Postmodernism, and Liberation Theology, their efforts rarely amount to more than, at best, labeling it Marxist and, at worst, declaring it vacuous. Both may be true, at least in principle, but neither approach fully refutes the driving force behind Critical Theory. And this doesn't even mention that most who have adopted Critical Theory activism don't know enough about its formulation themselves to even be conscious of its connection to Marxism. Instead, Critical Theorists tend to present complex modern arguments built upon logical fallacies regarding race, gender, socioeconomic status, and sexuality. By leveraging emotional reactions, social pressure, and societal guilt, the ideology of Critical Theory continues to gain ground in almost every facet of Western society—including the church and other Christian institutions.

Within Christendom, this is complicated even further. Woke Christians turn to the scriptures for proof texts to verify certain aspects of Critical Theory and Liberation Theology. They will use references to Jesus being a refugee[16] to give credence to open borders; Christ overturning the tables in the temple in order to support riots and protests;[17] and even twist Christ's intimate friendship with the Apostle John in an attempt to affirm the LGBTQ agenda and saying, "Jesus may well have been homosexual."[18] This selective use of scripture allows Critical Theorists to pick and choose parts of the canon that assist their cause while easily dismissing verses as outdated, out of context, or poorly translated that would harm their heretical positions.

From the outset, it should seem odd that Critical Theory and Christianity have become bedfellows. The humanist nature of Critical Theory (which depicts the human experience as the central aspect to existence as opposed to the Christ-centric view of Christianity) would seemingly create a conflict between the two. This obvious sharp contradiction, though, was rounded over time, like a stone slowly shaped by a stream, through the evolutionary development of Critical Theory.

While orthodox-minded Christians may have initially fled from versions of Critical Theory presented by radicals like Marcuse,[19] more modern kerygmatic Christian figures (e.g., Eric Mason,[20] Tony Campolo, Barry Corey, David Platt, LaCrae, and Andy Stanley[21]) have offered a softer, more subtle version of Jesus *and* Critical Theory. This version is what has found sympathetic ears among evangelicals. This new faith-based Wokeism didn't just originate overnight, nor did it leap unmolested from Marx to Mason. Rather, it evolved over time and across many different camps, both spiritual and secular, as ideological transmission took place. It migrated from Hegel and Marx to the Frankfurt School, to Black Liberation Theologians like James Cone, to Black feminists like Pauli Murray and Angela Davis, to modern Christ-touting Leftists like Jim Wallis and Michael Wear.[22] Then it jumped to more surprising sources, like VeggieTales creator Phil Vischer and Beth Moore,[23] before gaining the momentum and social receptivity among Christians that it has today.

Speaking to the overarching evolution of postmodern ideals that drive current iterations of Critical Theory, authors Helen Pluckrose and James Lindsay wrote:

> Since its revolutionary beginnings, postmodernism has
> evolved into new forms, which have preserved its original
> principles and themes, while gaining increasing influence
> over culture, activism, and scholarship, especially in the
> humanities and social sciences. Understanding postmodern-
> ism is therefore a matter of some urgency precisely because
> it radically rejects the foundations upon which today's
> advanced civilizations are built and consequently has the
> potential to undermine them.[24]

The evangelical church, although it rejected early versions of postmodernity, took quite seriously the importance of understanding postmodern culture. So much so that it seemed like nearly every Christian conference of the late 1990s and early 2000s featured speakers like Leonard Sweet, Rob Bell, and Doug Pagitt, who were dedicated to assisting the church in ministering to a new generation shaped by a postmodern mind-set. Interestingly, though, many of these individuals, especially Bell, who had a very public departure from evangelicalism,[25] and Pagitt, who proudly labels himself "a leading voice for Progressive Christianity"[26] and currently serves as the executive director for Vote Common Good,[27] a left-wing activist group that trains "democratic candidates to connect with Evangelical and Catholic voters,"[28] focused so much on transforming the church to reach postmoderns, that it seems they abandoned the original tenets of Christian faith and became postmodern themselves.

Like the men of Issachar, Bell and others "understood the times,"[29] but they erred. Failing to heed Paul's advice to the Galatian church—"if someone is caught in a sin, you who live by the Spirit should restore that person gently. But watch yourselves, or you also may be tempted,"[30]—instead of deconstructing *culture* to better align with the truth, they deconstructed *faith* in order to better reach the culture.

Bell, Pagitt, and other cultural architects ended up as Woke victims themselves, falling prey to the same philosophy they started out rebuking in the first place. By itself, this would be a tragedy, but it's compounded as leaders have led thousands down similar paths. Like the Pharisees in Matthew 23, these men are "blind guides" and are shaping others, as the church moves further and further away from the truth, into "twice as much a child of hell"[31] as they are. In order to protect the church, we must expose the deception!

The Systematic Theology of Wokeism

Michael Gungor, a formerly popular Christian artist who once boasted about losing followers on Twitter after recommending one of Bell's books,[32] wrote in a 2021 tweet: "Jesus was Christ. Buddha was Christ. Muhammad was Christ. Christ is a word for the Universe seeing itself. You are Christ. We are the body of Christ." While absent of any mention of typical Woke language (such as race, gender identity, microaggressions, intersectionality, or sexual orientation), Gungor's tweet is a perfect illustration of the systematic theology of Critical Theory and the corresponding Gnostic Hegelianism at the bedrock of Woke Christianity.

According to late eighteenth-century German philosopher Georg Wilhelm Friedrich Hegel, God, or what he interchangeably calls "Spirit," "Absolute Being," or "the Eternal," is "devoid of self" and "a long way yet from being the Spirit that knows itself as Spirit." Rather than being defined by orthodox Christian descriptors like "holy," "perfect," or "righteous," Hegel's god is clothed in imperfection and not yet fully realized or conscious of its Spiritness—or as Hegel describes it, as still in "the process in which Spirit becomes what it is in itself; and it is only as this process of reflecting itself into itself that it is in itself truly Spirit."[33]

Within Hegelian thought, the process of the Spirit knowing itself, or seeing the "primal Light" within itself, is realized at the culmination of the end of history, as all of the Spirits (Hegel appears to believe in more than one) unite and are reborn in a "new existence, a new world and a new shape of the Spirit."[34]

This eschatological event, according to Hegel, is unable to reach self-actualization, until mankind (whom Hegel calls "the universal divine Man" or "the community") becomes reconciled to the Spirit. Once this happens, it initiates a mystical union, much like a Communist utopia, in which the world is "implicitly reconciled with the divine Being."[25]

Hegel believed that this union between the Spirit and man will take place once humanity reaches such a state of perfection that the divine Being is able to recognize itself within the community of man. Once that takes place, man and Spirit shall be reunited and achieve oneness.

For Hegel, as long as there was ideological conflict present in the world, reconciliation with the divine Being wasn't possible. Ultimately, Hegel's mystical pursuit of universal agreement effectuated what we affectionately know as cancel culture. Inspired by Hegel, Herbert Marcuse wrote in his chilling 1965 essay "Repressive Tolerance": "Tolerance is extended to policies . . . which should not be tolerated because they are impeding, if not destroying, the chances of creating an existence without fear and misery."[36] For Marcuse, this meant silencing "false words and wrong deeds which demonstrate that they contradict and counteract the possibilities of liberation."[37]

What are the false words and wrong deeds according to Marcuse? He leaves no room for confusion:

> Liberating tolerance, then, would mean intolerance against movements from the Right, and toleration of movements from the Left.

In other words, true "tolerance" offers no tolerance at all toward differing opinions—especially if said opinions are conservative. While we'll speak to this more in future chapters, the important aspect to take away for now is understanding that ideological suppression isn't political nor arbitrary. Rather, it's mystical and theological—a reversing of the Tower of Babel, in essence, until we all speak one uniform and harmonizing Leftist language capable of ushering in a Gnostic utopia.[38]

To bring about this perfected society, Hegel (and later Marx) applied a unique argument, known as the "Hegelian Dialectic," which maintains that progress is derived from conflict. For Hegel, this conflict exists in the relationships among thesis, antithesis, and synthesis, or what Hegel called the "speculative."[39] Founder of New Discourses, James Lindsay, brilliantly unpacks Hegel's *modus operandi*, which he calls "the operating system of the Left," in his lecture "Hegel, Wokeness, and the Dialectical Faith of Leftism":

> So what Hegel actually means by "speculative" is having mystical content. It's mystical, it's mysticism . . . so this is going to open the door to a lot of things for Hegel that he already was—like hermeticism, alchemy and in particular also Gnosticism—which is why all of these ideologies like Critical Race Theory can be thought of as "Race Gnosticism," like people having a particular race because of their structurally determined lived experience, have special insight under a doctrine of standpoint epistemology[40] that gives them the ability to understand things and have racial

knowledges, etc.—that gives them special knowledge. That's Gnosticism, that's racial or ethnic Gnosticism ... because the Hegelian faith is itself gnostic."[41]

Hitting the nail on the head, Lindsay rightly exposes not only the Hegelian roots of Wokeism but, more importantly, the Gnostic substructure that shaped its development and continued evolution. Marx, who is most often associated with Critical Theory today, belonged to the Young Hegelian school of thought and while he maintained Hegel's use of the dialectic, criticized Hegel for his focus on mysticism and more spiritual themes. Marx wrote in 1873: "My dialectic method is not only different from the Hegelian, but is its direct opposite."[42]

For Marx, Hegel's work was rooted too much in idealism for his atheistic worldview and thus insufficient for bringing about the societal transformation he desired. As a result, Marx viewed the Hegelian dialectic as "standing on its head"[43] and felt it "must be turned right side up again, if you would discover the rational kernel within the mystical shell."[44]

Albert Mohler[45] describes Marx's process of standing Hegel's work on its head:

He saw capitalism as the thesis. He then saw a form of revolution, even a violent revolution, as the antithesis. The synthesis that he promised that would inevitably come out of a communist revolution would be a communist utopia. After the thesis would come the revolutionary antithesis and after the antithesis would come a new era of prosperity and peace under the rule of the people known as the Soviets.[46]

Between both views, the Hegelian and Marxist, lies the framework for the two major camps of Critical Theorists today—the spiritual and the secular.

Liberal academic theorists, diversity-obsessed sociologists, and left-wing educators pushing CRT in schools, tend to lean more toward a neo-Marxist position that replaces socioeconomic classes (proletariat vs. bourgeois) with categories of race (Black vs. White). But while Critical Theorists within Woke churches share the same race-based categories of secular theorists, they favor a more mystical Hegelian outlook overall, or what Lindsay describes above as "ethnic Gnosticism."

This is a perfect term for exactly what took place at St. Xavier Catholic Church in New York City during a mass in 2020, in which Father Kenneth Boller led his church in a question-and-response, uplifting diversity and denouncing White privilege, with questions like:

- Do you support racial justice, equity, and compassion in human relations?
- Do you affirm that White privilege is unfair and harmful to those who have it and to those who do not?
- Do you affirm that White privilege and the culture of White supremacy must be dismantled wherever it is present?
- Therefore, from this day forward, will you strive to understand more deeply the injustice and suffering White privilege and White supremacy cause?
- Will you strive to eliminate racial prejudice from your thoughts and actions, so that you can better promote the racial justice efforts of our church?[47]

Nowhere to be found within Boller's liturgical questions is any mention of the Gospel, grace, unconditional love, forgiveness, or the saving power of Jesus Christ. Instead, what is offered are the basic tenets of a secret Woke dogma that must be adhered to in order to be "saved" and accepted by the Woke Church, or in other words, ethnic Gnosticism.

The Gnostic Roots of Wokeism

At the end of the first century, after surviving both persecution and political pressure, the early Christian church faced a unique threat to the future of orthodoxy: the Gnostics. The term originates from the Greek word for knowledge (*gnosis)* and was a disparaging label fastened to the heretical group by the early church meaning "those who know."[48] This ancient religious movement, often erroneously intermingled with Jewish and Christian ideas, was unapologetically esoteric and imaginative, filled with a vast mythology of multiple heavens, an evil demiurge and a flawed creation. Highlighting the Gnostics' general dissatisfaction with the world, theologian and author Philip J. Lee writes:

> The ancient gnostic, looking at the world through despair-
> ing eyes, saw matter in terms of decay, place in terms of lim-
> itation, time in terms of death. In light of this tragic vision,
> the logical conclusion seemed to be that the cosmos itself—
> matter, place, time, change, body, and everything seen, heard,
> touched or smelled—must have been a colossal error.[49]

Like Critical Theory today, Gnosticism saw the material world as a corrupt fallen system full of conflict. Whereas modern Critical Theorists and Woke Christians see this system as a byproduct of a perceived White hegemony, ancient Gnostics believed this corruption was instigated by the Demiurge, the creative deity they associated with the Hebrew god Yahweh.

> All the Gnostic texts, though they differ in details, declare
> that we are strangers, aliens, sparks of Light or Spirit
> trapped in evil matter. They recount the cosmic process
> whereby the circles of the world have been created, by igno-
> rant or evil creators and *not* by the Light, and whereby we
> have become entrapped in the midmost or deepest dungeon.
> Finally, they impact the knowledge needed to escape back to

the one Light whence we have come and which is our real home.[50]

Within the Gnostic framework above, three key ideas are presented:

1. Alienation.
2. Man is trapped by an ignorant or evil creator/system.
3. Knowledge or revelation is required to awaken the truth or light within.

While each of these ideas originated within Gnosticism, they eventually found a welcomed place within a Hegelian/Marxist framework and continue to find a home in Wokeism.

Philosophical System	Alienation	Ignorant or Evil Creator/System	Knowledge/ Work Required
Gnostic Thought	Alienated by creation	Yaweh	Gain secret knowledge and recognize light inside
Hegelian Thought	Alienated by ourselves	Creation	Absolute Consciousness
Marxist Thought	Alienated by religion and class	Capitalism/ Bourgeoisie	Dismantle capitalism and allow communism to rise
Woke Thought	Alienated by racism and an existing moral and cultural framework	White hegemony	Awaken to systematic racism and do "the work" to become antiracist; engage in activism

Differences undoubtedly exist between Gnosticism and the philosophies of Hegel, Marx, modern Critical Theorists, and even Woke Christians. But in order to understand how Wokeism has developed within Christianity, it's important that we recognize the evolutionary pathway that Wokeism followed as it developed. To fail to make the connection between Wokeism and Gnosticism, even if one understands the latter influence of Hegel, is to fail to identify fully the heretical nature of Conscious "Woke" Christianity. While the aspects of modern Wokeism may be different today, the building blocks of alienation, systemic oppression, and a works-based enlightenment originated within the Gnostic heresy 2,000 years ago.

Outside of the church, Wokeism attracts a more Marxist view, with a highly antagonistic belief against God and religion. This requires finding a source to blame for the problems of humanity, including alienation and systemic oppression, other than the Almighty. In traditional Marxism, Marx found the perfect candidate in the Bourgeoisie, a perceived villainous middle class who "owned the means of production." But secular Woke theorists exchanged and modernized the view of the bourgeoisie for capitalism and a White hegemony, which includes a perceived man-made Eurocentric view of the Christian faith, which they hold responsible for creating a systematic objection against socialism, sexual liberation, and identity politics. Drawing from each of these systems, Wokeism within the church presents a noticeably Gnostic theology, complete with emphasis on alienation, systemic oppression, and works-based enlightenment.

Political philosopher Eric Voegelin felt that "Gnostic mass movements," like what we are witnessing today, were inevitable in a widely Christian society. He explains, "We are confronted with the singular situation that Christian faith is so much the more threatened the further it expands socially, the more it brings men under institutional control and the more clearly its essence is articulated."[51]

This trend toward Gnosticism is not due to a weakness in Christianity itself, but rather how it exposes the weakness in others. Describing how Christians drift toward Gnosticism, Voegelin wrote:

Coincidentally with its greatness, its weakness became apparent: great masses of Christianized men who were not strong enough for the heroic adventure of faith became susceptible to ideas that could give them a greater degree of certainty.[52]

While Christians might object to the idea that Voegelin suggests that Gnosticism appears more "certain" than faith in Christ, we must remember that "we live by faith, not by sight."[53] The Christian Gnostic, in contrast, focuses not on faith, but on knowledge and carnal works, and seeks escape from this world in mystic ritual rather than in spiritual and physical deliverance.

Part of the deception of Gnosticism, percolating all the way down to Woke Christianity, is how easily it is mistaken for orthodoxy by untrained minds.

Dr. Edward Feser, building upon Eric Voegelin's definitive work on the subject, refers to the "Hydra's head of modernist projects"[54] such as "liberalism, socialism, communism, scientism, progressivism, identity politics, globalism, and all the rest"[55] as "apostate projects"[56] that could only have "arisen in the midst of Christian civilization with the aim of supplanting it."[57]

Feser rightly concludes that Gnosticism, as well as Critical Race Theory and other Woke doctrines, were only possible within an existing Christian system because "they are all founded on some idea inherited from Christianity (i.e., the dignity of the individual, human equality, a law-governed universe, a final consummation, etc.) but removed from the theological framework that originally gave it meaning and radically distorted in the process."[58]

In this way, Gnosticism, from the first-century variety to today's Critical Race Theory, is a theological parasite becoming drunk on the doctrinal lifeblood of the Christian faith, before hatching its heretical progeny.

Mani and the Luminous Christ

Born in 216 AD in Babylonia, a decade before the fall of the Parthian Empire, rose a young prophet named Mani, whose teachings would posthumously shape followers from China to Rome through widespread missionary efforts. His teachings would eventually represent "one of the most pernicious forms of Christian heresy"[59] to ever exist.

Manichaeism, as it would eventually be called, was an elaborate religion amalgamated with adopted teachings from Buddhism and Zoroastrianism, layered upon Mani's own Gnostic Jewish-Christian upbringing. The result was a somewhat Christian-sounding faith, clouded by a robust dualistic cosmogony detailing the struggle of the spiritual world of light and the material realm of darkness, giving birth to what Mani believed was the perfect religious system.

According to Mani, God is not omnipotent but rather co-eternal with evil, caught in a cosmic stalemate with the "Prince of Darkness," a quintipartite demon-like creature "which had the head of a lion, the body of a dragon, the wings of a bird, the tail of a great fish and the feet of a beast of burden."[60] Additionally, the Manichaeans possessed a complex creation story permeated with vivid battles among multiple deities and forces of darkness and light, the formation of 10 heavens and eight earths from the bodies and skin of slayed demons, as well as an obscure narrative of the creation of Man.

Unlike the Genesis account, where "God formed a man from the dust of the ground and breathed into his nostrils the breath of life, and the man became a living being,"[61] the Manichaeans described Adam (and Eve) as being conceived by the copulation of two evil demons. As such, both the heavens and the earth, as well as humanity itself, were formed out of mostly evil materials that had "swallowed"[62] elements of light. Christ, then, was forced to take on the identity of "Jesus the Luminous" where "his primary role was as supreme revealer and guide and it was he who woke Adam from his slumber and revealed to him the divine origins of his soul and its painful captivity by the body and mixture with matter."[63]

Likewise, a similar belief exists within modern Woke Christianity: Man is trapped within an evil system, dependent upon God to show him that he is oppressed by this physical world and needs to become "Woke" in order to find salvation. On the surface, this may sound similar to a salvific message shared by Paul: "Wake up, O sleeper, rise from the dead, and Christ will shine on you,"[64] but as we will see, the Gnostic Gospel of Wokeism has little in common with the biblical message of the Christ crucified.

CHAPTER 2

The Historical Jesus

"Who Do Men Say I Am?"

"I cannot understand why scholars have a problem with Jesus knowing who He was . . . I would be more confused if He did not know
who He was,"[1] wrote American Catholic priest and author Joseph F.
Girzone, in his esteemed book *A Portrait of Jesus*. Girzone hits at the
heart of one of the longest debates within Christianity regarding the
identity of Christ; namely, *Who was Jesus?*

During the first few centuries AD, debates raged among Christians
regarding the specific nature of Jesus. Most doctrines fell within
one of two major camps: the Alexandrian school of thought, which
emphasized the divine and, at times, mystical nature of Christ, and
the Antiochene school, which asserted that Christ had two natures
within Him—one human and one divine. Extremism existed in
both camps, resulting in blatant heresies, such as Apollinarianism[2]
and Nestorianism.[3] But behind each of these complex theological
variations was a simple desire to make sense of the Carpenter from
Nazareth.

Since Jesus first inquired of Peter in Matthew 16, "Who do people say the Son of Man is?" mankind has been faced with the same question. Most evangelicals have confidently sided with Peter, who, when asked by Jesus, proudly proclaimed, "You are the Messiah, the Son of the living God." And although the traditional Christian response often revolves around ideas such as "Jesus is Lord," or "Jesus is fully human and fully God," or "Jesus is the second person of the Trinity," for others, the nature of Jesus has not been so black and white.

Not content with what they perceived to be the "blind faith" of orthodox Christians, skeptics, unbelievers, and heretics have always been happy to invent new ways of perceiving Christ, positing theories that include: Jesus was a man adopted by God (adoptionism), Jesus was a spiritual apparition (i.e., Docetism), and Jesus was a divine being created by God and subordinate to Him (subordinationism), while others assert that Jesus simply did not exist at all.

For these imaginative souls, Jesus might be a good teacher, a socialist, a charlatan, or even a fictitious creature altogether, but He certainly isn't the Christ. G. K. Chesterton once described such individuals as "men entangled in the forest of their own mythology . . . drowned in the sea of their own metaphysics."[4]

While examples of men wrestling with the doctrines of Christ can be found throughout the history of the church, perhaps no more poignant illustration of this phenomenon exists than among the cacophony of divergent views of Jesus that emerged among the liberal theologians of the eighteenth and nineteenth centuries. Only by understanding their pronounced departure from a belief in the divinity of Jesus will we be able to comprehend the evolution of the Woke Church of the twenty-first century.

The Birth of Critical Theology

Emerging from the aftermath of the philosophical influence of Kant and Hegel was a new form of religious discipline, which became known as Critical Theology. Carved by the writings of pioneers in the field like Hermann Samuel Reimarus,[5] Johannes Weiss, David Strauss, and Albert Schweitzer, these individuals worked to "demythologize" the scriptures and to construct a historical, rather than theological, profile of the "true" Jesus.

Jesus's biographers of this period argued that as long as an emphasis was placed on the miracles of Jesus, then the genuine biographical details of Jesus would not be uncovered. One such biographer, Albert Schweitzer, famously labeled these attempts to understand Jesus as "the quest of the Historical Jesus."[6] Schweitzer claimed that only by the absolute removal of all miraculous elements of the ministry of Jesus could the quest for the Historical Jesus be accomplished.

As such, the initial attempts to construct a historical record of Jesus meant that a predetermined set of criteria must exist before a proper understanding of Jesus could be established. But as professor of New Testament at Asbury Theological Seminary Craig S. Keener pointed out, "the radical Enlightenment's prejudice against divine or supernatural causation"[7] dramatically impacted the results of the corresponding historical research of the life of Jesus. Keener adds that such biographers risked "distorting and malforming what we know about Jesus"[8] through their attempts to carve Jesus into the reflection of their sociological and scholarly assumptions.

As a result, the criteria these Critical Theologians used to understand Jesus were from the start riddled with problems. Schweitzer himself concedes that "no historical school has ever laid down canons for the investigation"[9] of a historical profile for the life of Jesus outside the study of scripture itself.

Thus, the quest (which resulted in literally hundreds of "Lives of Jesus" as they became known) had to invent "its own methods"[10] for researching the life of Jesus that often required "historical imagination"[11] based on the far-reaching hypotheses and personal biases of each writer.

While Schweitzer's work arguably maintained a somewhat higher degree of historical scholarship than most, exhibited in his frequent sharp criticisms of others' versions of the Lives of Jesus, the majority of so-called early scholars in this field failed to evoke anything resembling historical research. Rather, what was produced was replete with ridiculous speculations regarding the divinity of Christ, in attempts to rationalize other causations for such miraculous events.

Reimarus, a professor of Oriental languages and a Deist who died in 1768, is widely recognized as one of the first to produce "a historical concept of the life of Jesus."[12] His work, published posthumously by Gotthold Ephraim Lessing and known collectively as "Fragments from Reimarus," contained a series of writings, including "The Aims of Jesus and His Disciples." Schweitzer called it "a masterpiece of general literature"[13] and "one of the greatest events in the history of criticism."[14] Keener, author of the exhaustive work *The Historical Jesus of the Gospel*, disagreed, citing that "scholars regard most of Reimarus's views as wrong,"[15] calling the work "a polemic rather than an objective historical study."[16]

Reimarus, afraid to publish his contrarian views during his lifetime, believed a chasm existed between the teachings of Jesus and what he believed were the fraudulent writings of the disciples. Much like Woke Christians today, Reimarus's Jesus was a mortal, a Jew, and a prophet, not the savior presented by the apostles.

> It has hitherto been shown that the new system adopted by the Apostles, of a spiritual suffering Saviour, who was to arise from the dead, and after his ascension to return from Heaven with great power and glory, is false in its first main principle, namely, the resurrection of the dead. . . . Their [the disciples] proof of the resurrection and of their whole system . . . is made up of scolding and scoffing, distortion of Scripture sentences, false conclusions.[17]

Hardly the "masterpiece" Schweitzer considered it, Reimarus's work paved the way for other skeptics to speak out. "Yet once

Reimarus's work pried open previously repressed academic possibilities," wrote Keener, "some others soon joined attempts to explain the
Gospel tradition without regard to the miracle claims so offensive to
the radical Enlightenment understanding of 'reason.'"[18]

The Lives of Jesus

Christians are no strangers to speculative criticism regarding the life
of Christ. In today's culture, a highly emotive, strongly opinionated,
and often biblically illiterate framework shapes a myriad of predict-
able and combative views against Biblical Christianity, such as:

- Jesus was actually married.
- The Bible isn't trustworthy.
- Jesus wasn't real.
- Bible translations have been altered.
- Jesus was gay or transgender.[19]
- Jesus didn't really rise from the dead.

As modern Critical Theologians, and their often less-informed
and Left-leaning Twitterati, opine wildly creative and sometimes
nearly comical theories regarding the Bible and the life of Jesus,
these individuals aren't the first to make such ludicrous claims about
the Son of God.

Perhaps the most ridiculous were the spurious writings of
German scholar Karl Friedrich Bahrdt, who theorized that the only
way to explain away the miraculous ministry of Jesus was to intro-
duce a conspiratorial view that Jesus, along with John the Baptist,
was a member of the secret society of Essenes. According to Bahrdt,
the order had undisclosed members in every corner of public life,
including the Sanhedrin. Interestingly enough, the goal of the Order
was to demolish the national faith of the Jews, by elevating the minds
of the people to higher spiritual truth. As a member of the Order,

Jesus was the "tool" the secret Essenian group used to deconstruct the Jewish establishment and enact a cultural and spiritual reset.

In Bahrdt's imagination, Luke, a physician and disciple of Christ, was also a member of the Order and used his advanced medical knowledge to teach Jesus how to cure coma patients and other serious ailments, which easily dismissed any accounts of miraculous healing in the New Testament. Luke's role also resurfaced for Bahrdt in the death, burial, and "resurrection" of Jesus. The German theologian, who was a member of a secret society himself (the Freemasons),[20] held that the crucifixion of Jesus was in fact a strategic plan carried out by the Essene Order to eradicate any remaining belief in a national Messiah. To complete the ruse, Luke gave Jesus a powerful drug to help Him endure pain and give the appearance of certain death. The plan also required bribing the centurion who pierced Jesus's side and another member of the Essene cult to dress up as an angel in order to announce Jesus's resurrection. Even more outrageous were Bahrdt's theories that Jesus fed the 5,000 with the assistance of several Essenian brothers who hid bread in a cave nearby and discreetly handed it to Him to pass out and that Jesus "walked on water" by floating on a giant raft across the raging sea.

While Bahrdt's work is only one example among hundreds of other Lives of Jesus, it demonstrates an exaggerated attempt to transform Jesus from a spiritual savior to a social reformer. In the end, even Albert Schweitzer, the most well-known Jesus biographer of his day, labeled Bahrdt's work fictitious,[21] but this didn't stop him from praising it as "a bold attempt to paint the portrait of Jesus Himself."[22] Fabricated as it was, Bahrdt's work inspired other more rational biographers like German professor Heinrich Paulus.[23]

Though born into a Christian home, Heinrich's father, a deacon in their church, was tormented over the doctrine of eternal life and believed he communicated with "departed spirits."[24] Paulus, negatively impacted by his father's spiritualism, developed a rationalistic view of miracles, believing them to be associated simply with poorly understood laws of nature rather than God's supernatural involvement. Paulus inevitably upheld Bahrdt's view of the miraculous, fortified by a greater appreciation for the sciences. As such, Paulus's Jesus didn't raise anyone from the dead; He simply saved them from "premature burial."[25] This included Jairus's daughter, Lazarus, and ultimately Jesus Himself, whom Paulus believed was rescued from a "death-like trance" by a great storm and a timely earthquake that woke Him back to consciousness.[26]

Bahrdt's and Paulus's accounts, and others like them, provided limited scholarly evidence for the alternative human Jesus sought by rationalists and Critical Theologians. In fact, later Historical Jesus biographer and member of the Jesus Seminar (which we'll discuss shortly) John Dominic Crossan called works such as theirs "an academic embarrassment," stating, "It is impossible to avoid the suspicion that Historical Jesus research is a very safe place to do theology and call it history, to do autobiography and call it biography."[27]

While Schweitzer's work exposed and did much to silence the unsound scholarship of contemporary "Jesus" biographers, his own conclusions initiated a unique damage to the faith all its own. Schweitzer believed that through the process of literary criticism, not rationalization, the Historical Jesus, once lost, could now be found.

"We must be prepared," warned Schweitzer, "to find that the Historical knowledge of the personality and life of Jesus will not be a help, but perhaps even an offence to religion."[28] This offense, for Schweitzer, came in the form of his historical presentation of Jesus as an eschatological or end-time prophet, who held a messianic consciousness; believing that His death would bring about the end of the world. Thus, Schweitzer's Jesus died a martyr but possessed no divinity.

What Does the Bible Say About the Quest for the Historical Jesus?

All of the various attempts by eighteenth- and nineteenth-century biographers to locate the Historical Jesus had three collective premises:

1. Historical facts are greater than Christian tradition.
2. Historical facts must be tested by skepticism.
3. No historical fact can contain any miraculous or supernatural event.[29]

Jacob Neusner rightly addressed these three commonalities in "Who Needs 'The Historical Jesus'?" and went even further, saying that all the advocates for the Historical Jesus begin "with the denial of the facticity of the Gospels."[30] As he goes on to demonstrate, the premises of the quest create a forced departure from a biblical worldview before the quest even sets sail by criticizing the authority of Christian tradition, accusing the Gospel writers of falsity, as well as denying any potential for a historical finding that could validate the lordship of Jesus.

Rather than a legitimate scholarly survey, the quest begins with an end in mind—a human Jesus. Like a scientist determined to make a discovery only to verify their biases, the writers of the quest left zero hope of discovering anything other than the Jesus whom they wanted to find, or as Neusner put it, "pretty much every scholar comes up with the Historical Jesus that suits his taste and judgment."[31]

Seemingly foreign to those on the quest are Paul's words:

> All Scripture is God-breathed and is useful for teaching,
> rebuking, correcting and training in righteousness, so that
> the servant of God may be thoroughly equipped for every
> good work.[32]

With that in mind, what good work has this quest produced in the world, or even in the church? Absent from the quest, according to Neusner, is any "determinative truth, vastly enriching the intellectual resources of the faith." Nowhere is this more obvious than in the end of Schweitzer's writings, where he left his readers with the astonishingly unhelpful conclusion that Jesus is nothing more than "one unknown," a man "without a name."[33]

Biblically speaking, the true Jesus is the polar opposite of Schweitzer's theological conclusion. Scripture is not shy at all about naming Jesus, nor revealing His true identity. Here is just a brief list of the names and titles given to Jesus throughout the scriptures:[34]

Almighty (Revelation 1:8)
Alpha and Omega (Revelation 22:13)
Author and Perfecter of Faith (Hebrews 12:2)
Bread of Life (John 6:35)
Beloved Son (Matthew 3:17)
Bridegroom (Matthew 9:15)
Cornerstone (Psalm 118:22)
Creator (Colossians 1:16-17)
Deliverer (1 Thessalonians 1:10)
Faithful and True (Revelation 19:11)
Good Shepherd (John 10:11)
Great High Priest (Hebrews 4:14)
Head of the Church (Ephesians 1:22)
Holy Servant (Acts 4:29-30)
I Am (John 8:58)
Immanuel (Isaiah 7:14)
Judge of the Living and the Dead (Acts 10:42)
King of Kings (Revelation 17:14)
Lamb of God (John 1:29)
Light of the World (John 8:12)
Lord of All (Philippians 2:9-11)
Messiah (John 1:41)
Mighty One (Isaiah 60:16)
Our Hope (1 Timothy 1:1)
Our Peace (Ephesians 2:14)
Prophet (Mark 6:4)

Redeemer (Job 19:25)

Risen Lord (1 Corinthians 15:3-4)

Rock (1 Corinthians 10:4)

Sacrifice for Our Sins (1 John 4:10)

Savior (Luke 2:11)

Son of Man (Luke 19:10)

Son of the Most High (Luke 1:32)

Resurrection and the Life (John 11:25)

The Door (John 10:9)

The Way (John 14:6)

The Word (John 1:1)

True Vine (John 15:1)

Victorious One (Revelation 3:21)

Wonderful Counselor, Mighty God, Everlasting Father, Prince of Peace (Isaiah 9:6)

Why Does Critical Theology Reject the Lordship of Jesus?

To understand how Critical Theology, as a whole, rejects the Lordship of Jesus, it's important to realize that the quest for the Historical Jesus began in an attempt to save Christianity, not destroy it. Early Critical Theologians and Jesus biographers, fueled by the Enlightenment, saw their work as salvaging the vast benefits of the moral and ethical aspects of Christian doctrine, while dismissing any and all fantastical events in order to remove opportunity for "Christian" teachings to be rejected by their rational-minded peers.

A similar tactic was used recently by famed apologist William Lane Craig, known for his powerful defense of the Gospel, where he applied Critical Theology tactics in order to synthesize the first three chapters of Genesis with modern evolutionary science. In an article published by First Things, Craig points to "mytho-history" in order to locate "the Historical Adam":

Genesis presents a history of the world that is extremely short by ancient standards, bound tightly by father-son genealogies. We should not imagine that the genealogies contemplate the enormous leaps that would be necessary to bring them into harmony with what we know of the history of mankind; but neither should we imagine that they comprise purely fictitious characters. We can avoid these antitheses by understanding the brief history they chronicle as a mytho-history, not to be taken literally. . . . If Genesis 1–11 functions as mytho-history, then these chapters need not be read literally.[35]

Craig continues calling the origins of Adam, the talking serpent in the garden, the fall of man and the cherubim guarding the entrance back to Eden as, "clearly metaphorical or figurative in nature."[36]

To be fair, Craig is far from a card-carrying member of the Christian Left. As one of the most renowned Christian apologists, known for debates with atheists like Sam Harris and Christopher Hitchens, Craig is a brilliant defender of the faith. Based on his past writings, Craig clearly believes in the divinity of Christ, so it's important to not discredit all of his work. However, Craig's steering away from an orthodox reading of Genesis as history should be cause for great concern among evangelical Christians.

In this instance, Craig drifts on the issue of biblical inerrancy, as he adopts stratagems used by Critical Theologians to "save" Christianity, even if it means destroying aspects of it first. Craig may find more agreement with the atheists he debates by labeling the first 11 chapters of Genesis "mytho-history," but at what cost?

Mark Goodacre, a well-respected New Testament scholar and professor at Duke University's Department of Religion, recently addressed the reason for doctrinal drift among textual scholars and Critical Theologians. In his opinion, textual scholars, guided by Critical Theology, "are really frustrated archeologists" who put "too much faith" in the role of the scholar.[37] As he describes, these individuals spend their lives looking for something in a 2,000-year-old text. When their premises aren't found, it forces them to explore and rationalize alternative solutions to validate their life's work. For many, the Historical Jesus provides that alternative solution, sanctioning use of the scriptures, while allowing scholars to pick and choose the aspects of the text that benefit their hypotheses the most.

After Schweitzer, though, upholding a belief in the Historical Jesus became much harder. Mere "rational" explanations were exposed as shoddy scholarship, and the use of fictitious backstories to explain how Jesus performed miracles (e.g., "Jesus was in a secret society") were often rejected outright. This left the Critical Theologians in a bit of a conundrum.

Proving a Historical Jesus, one who was not divine, would be difficult from the surviving biblical text that clearly recounts a miracle-working Messiah, who died and rose from the dead on the third day, demonstrating His Lordship. If Jesus's biographers were to disprove the traditional Christian narrative, it would require an additional ancient source to trump the existing Gospel account and demonstrate that their version of Jesus was more accurate. Ultimately, Critical Theologians found this source in the "discovery" of the Gospel of Q.

The Gospel of Q

A decade before Schweitzer published his work *The Quest of the Historical Jesus* (1906), Critical Theologians stumbled upon what they believed to be the discovery of a lifetime—the Gospel of Q. In reality, this discovery wasn't a discovery at all; rather, it was a theorized belief in a pre-existent hypothetical lost Gospel, upon which the other Synoptic Gospel writers (Matthew, Mark, and Luke) relied heavily when writing their own accounts. If true, Q would contain the earliest source information of the sayings of Jesus and change the course of the quest for the Historical Jesus, as well as the understanding of Christianity, forever.

Rather than a landmark archaeological find, as were the Dead Sea Scrolls in 1947,[38] the belief in Q evolved over time. Until the nineteenth century, biblical scholars relied on Augustine's view that Matthew's Gospel was written first and was used by Mark and that Luke followed, using both Matthew and Mark as source material. By the nineteenth century, though, scholarship began to demonstrate that Mark's Gospel was penned first (known as the "Markan priority"), and that Matthew and Luke cross-referenced Mark when writing their own accounts,[39] thus explaining their significant commonalities.

If the Markan priority was true, though, what was the origin of the remaining material in Matthew and Luke that they did not have in common? Where did this come from? It was this question that gave rise to the idea of Gospel of Q. Specifically, the Gospel of Q theory asserted that Matthew and Luke drew not upon Mark's Gospel, as had been, thought, but upon a lost Gospel account.

The Q hypothesis was dialectically advanced by Critical Theologians to address these questions and more. Beginning with English bishop Herbert Marsh; Friedrich Schleiermacher, the known father of modern Liberal Theology; and Johannes Weiss, the term "Q" was used as an abbreviation of the German word *quelle*, meaning "source."

A major flaw in the argument for Q begs the question, "If Q was so accessible to Matthew and Luke, why are there no mentions of it in early Christian literature?" With the plethora of patristic writings that are available from the first and second centuries, one would expect at least a subtle tip of the hat to what is today believed to be the shaping document for the entire account of the life of Jesus. Yet, all early church fathers, including Jerome, Clement, Ignatius, Origin, and Irenaeus are silent on the issue. And despite zero historical references to substantiate its existence, Q is now treated "as part of the established literature of early Christianity."[40]

The Q hypothesis, without any physical evidence of its existence, without any mention in early church history, and without any trust-worthy reconstructions of it as a source, remains as a central linchpin for Critical Theologians and modern Jesus biographers as evidence for the Historical Jesus. As Keener points out, in many cases "the version of 'Q' some scholars are citing is essentially nothing more than a collection of sayings selected to fit their narrower reconstruc-tion of Jesus."[41]

One popular modern Critical Theologian, Bart Ehrman, not only relies on Q to peddle his best-selling books on the Historical Jesus as an apocalyptic prophet, but doesn't even hesitate to tell his readers what Q contained and what it didn't, as if it's a document he's actually read.

> It [Q] certainly had some of the most familiar sayings of
> Jesus. It contained . . . the Beatitudes and the Lord's Prayer;
> it included the commands to love your enemies, not to judge
> others, and not to worry about what to eat and wear; and it
> provided a number of familiar parables.[42]

Ehrman does eventually counsel readers on the limitations of Q as a non-surviving source, but only after applauding the "docu-ment" as being "chock-full of apocalyptic sayings on the lips of Jesus, sayings in which he predicts the imminent end of the age in a cata-strophic act of judgment."[43] Ironically, if Ehrman applied the same level of faith in Christ that he has in Q, he'd probably be a Christian. Unfortunately for Ehrman and the world, theologian Michael Bird reminds us that the Critical Theologian is currently far from making a confession of faith: "Ehrman is an evangelist for unbelief, enabling sceptics to keep their disgust with Christianity fresh, while trying to persuade believers that their cherished beliefs about Jesus are a house of Historical straw."[44]

The Jesus Seminar

Another group to rely heavily on Q is known as the Jesus Seminar. The Jesus Seminar began in 1985 when Robert Funk, who at one time served as the president of the Society for Biblical Literature, gathered together approximately 30 New Testament scholars to re-embark on the quest for the Historical Jesus. Over time, the Seminar grew to over 200 members, known as Fellows, most of whom were well-credentialed professors, lecturers, and researchers.

From 1985 to 1991, the group met to analyze all the sayings of Jesus, from every source available, to determine which sayings were "authentic" and which were fabricated or rooted in Christian myth. From 1991 to 1995, a similar study commenced concentrating on the deeds of Jesus, including miracles, to again determine "fact" from "fiction." Perhaps most bizarre, in order to vote on their viewpoint, each member would present a colored bead for every account. For instance, a red bead implied that Jesus "undoubtedly said this or something very like it,"[45] while a black bead would mean "Jesus did not say this."[46]

Unlike Schweitzer and Ehrman, the Historical Jesus uncovered by the Jesus Seminar was not found to be an end-times prophet but rather "a non-eschatological sage."[47] Like Ehrman, though, the Jesus Seminar relied on the nonexistent Q to provide the "earliest evidence for the Historical Jesus."[48] Using these findings, the Jesus Seminar put together its own Gospel account, called *The Gospel of Jesus*, detailing the fellows' "consensus on all the words and deeds of Jesus."[49]

Funk and his fellows surprisingly recognize more of Jesus's miraculous deeds than many of their earlier predecessors, but still absent from their text is any mention of Jesus walking on water, feeding the 5,000, or turning water into wine. In fact, leaving the biggest void from the biblical narrative is the exclusion of the resurrection story itself, with the final verse of *The Gospel of Jesus* containing nothing more than hopeless prose, "Jesus breathed His last."

The Building Blocks of Future Heresy

As Goodacre humbly acknowledges,[50] the one thing that almost all Critical Theologians share is a misplaced faith in the scholar.

Did Q exist? Were there additional sayings of Jesus compiled prior to our New Testament accounts? Perhaps. But after 2,000 years, we have no real way of knowing. What we do have, though, are 27 well-preserved and easily verifiable books of the New Testament detailing the life, death, burial, and resurrection of Jesus. If these weren't enough, we also have hundreds of rich early church writings, moving personal testimonies, and historical annals, such as Josephus and Tacitus, all validating the New Testament narrative and the absolute supremacy of the Lordship of Jesus the Christ.

Yet, taking all this into account, unbelieving scholars would rather rely on imaginative stories of floating rafts, secret societies, and fabricated source material than take real documented evidence at face value. In no other historical field of study would this behavior be tolerated, yet within Christianity, especially within Woke Christian academic institutions, not only is such poor scholarship not condemned, but it's granted the seat of honor at the table.

This isn't to say that all aspects of Critical Theology are bad. Insomuch as scholars remember that the task of textual analysis is to reclaim the purity of the original biblical account to ensure that believers have at their disposal the most refined tools for discipleship, translation, and faith-building as possible, such work will only serve to enhance the faith. But the moment we allow biases, agenda-driven scholarship, and the pursuit of the *what-could-be* to take precedence over *what is*, we are no longer doing the work of historical analysis but simply feeding the overactive imagination of a cultural and political Zeitgeist bent on hammering an additional nail into the cross of Christ.

As C. S. Lewis wrote:

> You must make your choice. Either this man was, and is, the Son of God: or else a madman or something worse. You can

shut Him up for a fool, you can spit at Him and kill Him as a demon; or you can fall at His feet and call Him Lord and God. But let us not come with any patronising nonsense about His being a great human teacher. He has not left that open to us. He did not intend to.[51]

Beyond the personal consequences of rejecting Jesus's divinity, which Lewis so eloquently reminds us of, the biased quest for the Historical Jesus of the eighteenth and nineteenth centuries initiated a landslide of heretical teachings that continue to bombard and confuse the Western church to this day. Without the quest, Woke Christianity would arguably lack the theological building blocks necessary to stand on its own.

But as we will see in the next chapter, it was the Historical Jesus research that was utilized in Nazi Germany that caused Aryan Christianity to thrive. And long before there was Critical Race Theory, the Critical Theology movement empowered by the dialectical quest for the Historical Jesus gave birth to the racist dogmas of Black Liberation Theology.

CHAPTER 3

God and Race

Help Me to Hate White People

> Dear God, Please help me to hate White people. Or at least
> to want to hate them. At least, I want to stop caring about
> them, individually and collectively. I want to stop caring
> about their misguided, racist souls, to stop believing that
> they can be better, that they can stop being racist.[1]

Professor of practical theology at Mercer University Dr. Chanequa
Walker-Barnes had the above "prayer" to offer as a contribution to a
best-selling collection of prayers, *A Rhythm of Prayer: A Collection of
Meditations for Renewal.*

As you might imagine, Dr. Walker-Barnes's prayer, which continues in a like manner for another four pages, erupted in controversy. She was accused of peddling Critical Race Theory, Wokeness,
and racism against Whites. While all of these accusations against
her may be true, I heard something else in her words: piety. Not

Christian piety, of course, but a deep-rooted piousness and adherence to the writings of American theologian James Cone and his Gospel of Black Liberation Theology.

A victim of intense racial segregation during his upbringing in rural Arkansas, Cone drew upon his own experience, as well as the influence of controversial figures W. E. B. DuBois and Malcom X, to sculpt a theology that would address "the Black struggle for justice" from a Christian framework. For Cone, this meant a Black theology must "analyze the satanic nature of Whiteness"[2] and "prepare all non-Whites for revolutionary action."[3] Granting more authority to Black experience than both church tradition or scripture itself, Cone felt that "the spirit of the authentic Gospel is often better expressed by 'heretics' than by the 'orthodox' tradition."[4]

Unshackled from the weight of biblical orthodoxy and 2,000 years of Christian tradition by the works of DuBois and Malcolm X, Cone now had the ability to shape doctrine, apart from God, as he saw fit.

One area in which he did this was in his theology of sin. Instead of "missing the mark" of God's righteousness standard, Cone described: "In a word, sin is Whiteness—the desire of Whites to play God in the realm of human affairs."[5]

The only solution according to Black Liberation Theology was "the destruction of Whiteness, which is the source of human misery in the world." Within the Black community though, sin looked different.

For Blacks, Cone taught that there were only two main offenses against God:

1. To deny the reality of Black oppression.
2. Loving Whites and allowing them to define Black existence.

Understanding these two aspects of Black Liberation Theology allows us to comprehend the sincerity of Dr. Walker-Barnes as she prayed, "Dear God, Please help me to hate White people." To what degree she is consciously aware of her devotion to Cone's dogma is unclear, but regardless, her poem reveals how subversive Black Liberation Theology truly is, especially in religious circles.

The Theology of James Cone

"In order to be Christian theology, White theology must cease being White theology and become Black theology by denying Whiteness as an acceptable form of human existence and affirming Blackness as God's intention for humanity."[6] Inspired by Liberation Theology, a Marxist-infused faith that arose in Latin America during the 1950s, Cone reworked the oppressed-and-oppressor framework to address the hardships of Blacks in America. The resulting faith, known as Black Liberation Theology, elevated racial liberation over personal salvation.

"Jesus is not a human being for all persons," Cone boldly asserts. "He is a human being for oppressed persons, whose identity is made known in and through their liberation."[7] A far cry from the scriptural perspective that Christ "is the atoning sacrifice for our sins, and not only for ours but also for the sins of the whole world,"[8] Cone's first incarnation of the Woke Jesus was as "primarily a social reformer."[9] Liberated by Schweitzer's "Historical Jesus," Cone gained the analytical tools necessary to deconstruct the sources of "White religion" in order to develop a systematic theology for oppressed people.

In Christian theology, "sources" refers to the various authoritarian sources from which the church derives its meaning. These include first, and foremost, scripture, then church creeds, confessions, doctrinal statements, reason, and person revelation. While different denominations may debate the authority given to each type of source, most are in agreement that scripture is the *principium theologiae*, that is, the "norming norm," or the standard, by which all other sources are measured.

Black Liberation Theology, finding justification in the Barthian view[10] that separated God's revelation as independent from the written word of the Holy Scriptures, established new "sources" of authority to help liberate Blacks from oppression. Rejecting the traditional sources of Christian orthodoxy, Cone sought to uphold Black Liberation Theology through what he felt were more relevant sources. Those relevant sources? Black experience, Black culture, Black history, and the revelation of the Black Jesus.

Most important to Cone was the Black Jesus. Making his case for the Black Christ, Cone said, "This and this alone is the norm for Black-talk about God."[11]

The Black Christ

An accomplished theologian, Cone starts off well: "To speak of the Christian Gospel is to speak of Jesus Christ who is the content of its message and without whom Christianity ceases to be. Therefore the answer to the question 'What is the essence of Christianity?' can be given in two words: Jesus Christ."[12]

For Cone, though, this wasn't enough, as it didn't segregate how the person of Jesus viewed Black oppression. Therefore, Cone was forced to "investigate the meaning of His person and work in light of the Black perspective."[13] Thus, each aspect of Jesus's life—His birth, baptism, temptation in the wilderness, ministry, death, and resurrection—must be evaluated through a lens of race in order to understand and receive the revelation of the Black Christ.

This investigation led Cone to conclude that the Black Christ was the fulfillment of the quest for the Historical Jesus. So much so, Cone felt "any other statement about Jesus Christ is at best irrelevant and at worst blasphemous."[14] Cone explained that the "definition of Jesus as Black is crucial"[15] for all who were serious about their faith. As professor and theologian Dr. Owen Strachan elucidated regarding Cone in his book *Christianity and Wokeness*: "This truth rendered the 'Black' community free of 'White' theological influence." But in order to fully accomplish this, Black Liberation Theology had to crucify the "White Jesus."

"The White Jesus tries to convince us that there is no difference between American democracy and Christian freedom, that violence is no way to respond to inhumanity."[16] Embracing the spirit of Marxist revolution, Cone had no problem encouraging revolution against what he saw as a White hegemony, even if that meant violence:

The Black experience is the feeling one has when attacking the enemy of Black humanity by throwing a Molotov cocktail into a White-owned building and watching it go up in flames. We know, of course, that getting rid of evil takes something more than burning down buildings, but one must start somewhere.[17]

As if foreshadowing the riots during the summer of 2020 after the death of George Floyd at the hands of a Minneapolis police officer, Cone saw revolution through "whatever means necessary" as a form of God's revelation, assuring Blacks that "their work in their own liberation is God's own work."[18] Like Marx, Cone flipped the Gnostic views of Hegel of escaping alienation and oppression through enlightenment on their head, opting instead for a race-oriented proletarian revolution against White hegemony, both societal and theological. While activism, protest, and what Cone called "risky human encounters"[19] play a part in manifesting God's Black revolution against Whites, ultimately for it to be fully successful, Black theology must kill both God and White Jesus.

"Black theology must realize that the White Jesus has no place in the Black community, and it is our task to destroy Him. We must replace Him with the Black Messiah,"[20] Cone affirms. Similar to the ancient "Epic of Gilgamesh," where the hero Gilgamesh[21] seeks revenge against the immortal creature Huwawa,[22] after his ancestors are destroyed by flood, Cone's Black Liberation Theology seeks to slay the White Jesus as a retaliation against the systematic oppression of Blacks due to Jesus's "White religion."

Of course, no serious student of theology believes in a "White Jesus" in the literal sense. As evangelist Billy Graham put it, as a Middle Eastern Jew, Jesus "was not a White man. He was not a Black man. He came from that part of the world that touches Africa and Asia and Europe and He probably had a brown skin." More importantly, Graham concluded his point, offering, "Christ belongs to all people. He belongs to the whole world."[23]

Cone, as a well-educated man, surely understood this, but for him, the idea of a White Jesus encompassed much more than mere superficial pigmentation; it represented 2,000 years of a White religion that he felt was complicit in Black oppression. As such, Cone believed Black Theology must "break with traditional theological concerns"[24] in order to promote Black power. He confessed that "this interpretation of theology will seem strange to most Whites and even some Blacks" who may question whether Christ was truly Black, but this appeared to matter little to Cone, who was willing to abandon traditional theology, and even scripture itself, in order to promote his heretical and hate-filled version of the Christian faith.

The ironic fact lost on Cone, as well as on most Woke social justice warriors, is that a great number of the early patristic church fathers who had shaped what he referred to as "White religion," such as Augustine, Origen, Tertullian, Cyprian, and Athanasius, were all People of Color from various parts of Northern Africa. While this shouldn't matter, since Paul reminds us, "there is neither Jew nor Gentile, neither slave nor free,"[25] it's important as society experiences increasing racial tension that the true history of Christianity emerges to extinguish revisionists' lies about traditional Christianity.

Christianity has never been a White man's Gospel. It began on the day of Pentecost with "God-fearing Jews from every nation under heaven"[26] and culminates with "a great multitude that no one could count, from every nation, tribe, people and language, standing before the throne and before the Lamb."[27] While Christians can be sympathetic to the historical oppression of Blacks through slavery, segregation, the Ku Klux Klan, and Jim Crow laws, we cannot adhere to the race-based version of Christianity to which Cone ascribed.

Surprisingly, though, Cone wasn't the first to attempt to racialize Jesus and segregate Christians based on race and skin color. Several decades before Cone's Black Jesus would come to be, another false Christ was being perpetuated: the Aryan Jesus of Nazi Germany.

The Aryan Jesus

A year before James Cone was born, a group of pastors and theologians gathered at Wartburg Castle in Germany to recognize the inauguration of the Institute for the Study and Eradication of Jewish Influence on German Church Life. According to professor and author Susannah Heschel, the institute sought "to create a dejudaized church" for Nazi Germany, free of Jewish influence through "new biblical interpretations and liturgical materials."[28] In a strange parallel to Cone's Black Liberation Theology, the Nazi-infiltrated German Church sought to establish a Jesus in their image, an Aryan Jesus, to assist in liberating the German people from the, as they described, morally repugnant Jewish people. The Aryan Jesus, it was announced, "was not a Jew but an opponent of Judaism."[29]

To accomplish this, the Institute assisted Adolf Hitler and his National Socialist Party in purging Christianity of Semitic influence, including the Old Testament. The amputation of half the Bible, specifically the portion detailing God's covenant with Israel, proved not to be enough, though, to convert Jesus from the Jewish Messiah to an anti-Semite "Jewish Destroyer," so theologians were encouraged to teach scripture out of context and to "invent alternative originary narratives"[30] and use whatever means necessary to undermine Judaism's influence on the Christian faith.

This forced the Nazified German Church to look for influences outside of orthodox Christian faith to justify its dogma. Just as Cone relied on Marxism to construct Black Liberation Theology, theologians within Nazi Germany combined Germanic myths,[31] Norse mythology,[32] and even Indian Buddhism[33] in an effort to "reconstruct Christian origins and teachings as well as the use of Christianity to justify racist oppression and murder."[34]

Nazi Germany turned to theologians like Walter Grundmann, the academic director of the Institute; Kurd Niedlich, a Berlin schoolteacher and a cofounder of the League for German Churches (Bund für deutsche Kirche); and German protestant theologian Albert Kaltoff. Helping them to develop this unique German hybrid form of Christianity was a nineteenth-century tendency novelist, Berthold Auerbach, who used his fictional writings to shape the religious and moral beliefs of the people. Historian George L. Mosse details Auerbach's influence, stating:

> In Auerbach's writings the pantheistic life force took on
> religious overtones. Sketching one of the peasants as a "real
> German," Auerbach says of him that "even today he is a
> simple and just man, loyal and filled with faith." This faith
> which should be professed by the simple and just man was
> exemplified, in one of Auerbach's stories, by a person who
> ministered to the peasants' spiritual needs. A thoroughly
> good man, of a "pure and beautiful nature"—as Auerbach
> depicts him—the minister is unalterably opposed to
> Protestant orthodoxy, believing that true Christianity is sig-
> nified solely by the possession of a "sanctified heart." With
> his undogmatic faith, the person is able to tame even the
> wildest and most unruly peasants. . . . Whereas Auerbach's
> work represents only an early literary expression of the
> fusion of peasant virtues and faith, later Volkish[35] thought
> more explicitly combined the glorification of the peasant
> with a simple heartfelt religious, a Christianity not hemmed
> in by theological orthodoxy and thus free to fuse the life
> spirit originating in the pantheistic cosmos.[36]

The goal of this spiritual fusion, at least in how it eventually evolved within the Nazi party, was to protect and establish a racial purity among the German Volk, free from Jewish "oppression." As such, the Church of the Reich, as Mosse describes "not hemmed in by theological orthodoxy," was free to gather to itself pantheistic doctrines forbidding racial admixture, the appointment of Jews in church leadership, and evangelism to Jewish communities. Essentially, for the twisted logic of the German Church, a love of country and a love for God meant hatred toward the Jews.

The Jews, according to the Nazis, were inferior and parasitical in nature. They saw them as a toxic race living off the fortunes of other races, weakening the whole nation. Hitler believed them to be, along with the Christians, responsible for the fall of Rome, and as such, he was executing preventive justice by their removal and extermination—thus protecting the German Reich.

Christian Nationalism

A similar accusation has recently arisen against modern conservative Christians in America who hold both a love for God and love for country. Labeled with the term "Christian Nationalists," many believers are wrongly accused of fascist tendencies and a Nazi-like patriotic zeal. Perhaps the best example of this was the media outpouring after the Capitol riot on January 6, 2021.

Here are just a few of the headlines surrounding the incident casting blame on Christians:

- "How the Christian Right Helped Foment Insurrection"[37]
- "A horn-wearing 'shaman.' A cowboy evangelist. For some, the Capitol attack was a kind of Christian revolt."[38]
- "A Christian Insurrection"[39]
- "Militant Christian Nationalists Remain a Potent Force, Even After the Capitol Riot"[40]

- "Police officer says Jan. 6 insurrectionists 'perceived themselves to be Christians'"[41]
- "The Growing Anti-Democratic Threat of Christian Nationalism in the U.S."[42]

Among those pointing a finger toward conservative Christians is Andrew Whitehead, sociologist and co-author of the book *Taking America Back for God: Christian Nationalism in the United States*, who claims religion, specifically a right-wing Christian Nationalism, was "a key explanation" for the events surrounding the breach of the U.S. Capitol Building on January 6, 2021. Whitehead's broad categorization of Christian Nationalism includes anyone who "believe(s) either that the U.S. was or still is a Christian nation" and who possesses a desire to see the nation return to its foundational Christian values. According to Whitehead, Christian Nationalists can be identified through behaviors, such as encouraging Christian prayer before school sports, voting for, and support of, President Donald Trump, participating in evangelism, awaiting the Second Coming of Christ, and supporting Israel.[43]

Using Whitehead's definition, almost every evangelical Christian in America concerned with revival or reaching the lost could be accused of falling within this spectrum—which seems to be exactly Whitehead's goal.

After identifying the church as the villain, Whitehead then goes a step further in accusing these individuals of both Nativism and racism and justifying "violence in the service of what they deem the greater good or even God's plan." With his fabricated sociological profile, Whitehead goes on to hold Christians culpable for everything from racial injustice to police brutality and the spread of COVID-19.[44]

Vastly different from the Christian Nationalists within the Third Reich, the present-day believers identified by Whitehead are vilified, not for abandoning orthodoxy, but for upholding it. Rather than using the authority of the church to push the agenda of a *Führer*, Christian conservatives today focus on upholding dramatically countercultural ideals like protecting the nuclear family; rejecting unscientific (and unbiblical) views of gender and sexuality; proclaiming the equality of all people regardless of race, gender, or any other factor; as well as fighting for the freedom of speech, a free press, and fair elections for all.

In light of this, it could be argued that Woke Christians are the true "Christian Nationalists."

They have exchanged the divinity of Christ for a secular Jesus. They have willingly disconnected themselves from the inerrancy of the scriptures, embraced sinful views of gender and sexuality, have joined forces with Marxist groups (like Black Lives Matter and Antifa) in accusations against biblically minded conservatives, and pledged allegiance to an ever-increasing tyrannical socialist puppet government.

Take Ed Stetzer, progressive theologian and executive director of the Wheaton College Billy Graham Center, who felt compelled to march in solidarity alongside anarchists and Leftists[45] during the violent riots of 2020. Or perhaps Curtis Chang, founder of Redeeming Babel, in collaboration with known democratic operative and director of faith outreach for President Barack Obama Michael Wear,[46] who together launched the "Christians and the Vaccine" project,[47] a propaganda campaign aimed at increasing vaccination rates among evangelicals.

Another spiritual advisor to Obama, Joel Hunter, abandoned his once orthodox convictions to help institute the campaign "Pro-Life Evangelicals for Biden," claiming that the Democratic Party platform was more "biblically balanced."[48] Or propping up the progressives agenda is also the Reconciling Ministries Network, whose mission is to mobilize "United Methodists of all sexual orientations and gender identities to resist evil, injustice, and oppression in whatever forms they present themselves."[49] Likely the "evil" the Network resists includes biblically minded evangelical Christians

who reject the heretical position that the Bible affirms an LGBTQ
lifestyle.

As such, it's easy to see how evangelical Christians, who stand
firm against the false doctrines of the Woke Church, can quickly be
labeled as "evil" or "oppressive" by the Leftist state, as they are often
targeted and accused by the Democratic Party of being homophobic,
Islamophobic, and utilizing hate speech.

Even far-Left filmmaker and activist Michael Moore went
as far as to compare Southern Baptists to Afghanistan's Taliban.
Referencing the Taliban's unjust treatment toward females, he stated,

> They're religious nuts, but we've got those here too . . . they
> said yesterday in their press conference that girls' schools are
> going to remain open. OK. We'll see. They also said they are
> going to operate under Islamic law. That's exactly how a lot
> of Southern Baptists want it to be here too . . . we are fol-
> lowing dictates of conservative Christians. It's wrong there
> and it's wrong here.[50]

Falling shy of Moore's comparing evangelicals to terrorists, the
American Medical Association issued its own indictment against
conservative Christians at the end of 2020. The association chastised
the U.S. Supreme Court for declining to consider the likelihood of
COVID-19 spread during Christian worship services in its verdict
in favor of New York residents who had their First Amendment
rights violated by disgraced former New York governor Andrew
Cuomo, saying there was "no doubt" that Christian events spread
the coronavirus.[51]

Interesting enough, within Nazi Germany, the Jews were
blamed by Nazis for creating similar social and economic issues[52]
and for spreading diseases, like typhus.[53] As such, the German
people initially sought to limit the influence of the Jews through
the boycotting of Jewish-owned businesses and inevitably through
intimidation, physical harm, and eventually death. While, thankfully,

at the moment, the situation in America doesn't even compare to the atrocities experienced in Nazi Germany, there are many similarities.

When asked about how to address the issue of so-called Christian Nationalism, Whitehead ruminated that "Christian nationalism is predicated on power, and again, trying to maintain privileged access and control to power in the levers of power. And so it will respond to power."[54] Likely unknown to Whitehead, who admits he's "not an expert in Nazi Germany"[55] at its fundamental level, this was the driving philosophy used against the Jews in Germany.

According to the *Holocaust Encyclopedia*, the Nazis believed the Jews had too much power within society, which required a stronger force to be applied in opposition to them. Furthermore, Hitler expressed concern about the negative impact that traditional Christianity could also have on the Reich: "We'll see to it that the churches cannot spread abroad teachings in conflict with the interests of the State. We shall continue to preach the doctrine of National Socialism and the young will no longer be taught anything but the truth."[56]

Whereas Cone blamed "White theologians" for distorting the Black Christ's Gospel of liberation, the Führer felt that his Aryan Jesus was lost due to a "religion fabricated by Paul of Tarsus"[57]—that is, Christianity itself. In this unfounded view of Pauline influence on Christianity, Hitler and others believed that Paul leveraged and distorted the teachings of the Historical Jesus to create a societal uprising designed to liberate the Jews from Roman rule. Attempting to correct the position, Hitler affirmed, "Nevertheless, the Galilean, who later was called the Christ, intended something quite different. He must be regarded as a popular leader who took up His position against Jewry."[58]

Likewise, Woke Christians and progressive ideologues point judgmental fingers against biblically grounded evangelicals, for ultimately they must be silenced. For Whitehead, this involves "protecting democracy" against this wide-sweeping group of mostly White

Christian Nationalists in order to ensure "that the levers of power" don't fall into the wrong hands.[59]

Much like the German church's view of the Jews, progressive sociologists, like Whitehead, seem to imply that the Woke Jesus is the true redeemer of the people, while a belief in the biblical Jesus is destructive and, if allowed to propagate, may very well lead to the downfall of society. So while White evangelical Christians are commonly labeled by the media and Leftist political pundits as "Christian Nationalists," it is in fact Left-leaning Christian thinkers, like Chang or Hunter, who exhibit more matching characteristics of Christian Nationalism by pedaling progressive propaganda and anti-biblical notions in full agreement with the rising Leftist state.

This isn't to say that there aren't any examples of rogue (so-called) conservative Christian people committing injustices or heinous crimes against others, or even individuals who elevate flag over faith. But within Christian orthodoxy, the absolute theological norm maintains a primacy of God over country, scripture over state mandates, and the Lordship of Jesus Christ over any politician or political candidate (including even President Trump).

Surprisingly, Hitler himself affirmed this truth in response to Hanns Kerrl's, the Reichsminister of Church Affairs, attempts at trying to produce a Nazi/Christian hybrid: "Kerrl, with the noblest of intentions, wanted to attempt a synthesis between National Socialism and Christianity. I don't believe the thing's possible, and I see the obstacle in Christianity itself."[60]

New Allegiances

While Woke Christianity is somewhat unique from the Aryan Christian faith of the Nazis, or Cone's Black Liberation Theology counterpart, it demonstrates a similar pattern, as each adopted racist ideologies on top of an existing Christian substructure in order to establish its dogma. Woke Christianity is distinct from Black Liberation Theology in that it fails to go so far as calling for the destruction of Whiteness. But it's related to Black Liberation Theology in that it does also accuse Whites of racial fragility and places upon them the guilt of the totality of historical oppression against Blacks. In the same manner, Wokeism is not Aryan Christianity and should not be flippantly declared "Nazi," but neither should it be given a pass for its similar allegiance to the secular state and anti-Semitic views, especially in relationship to the Israeli–Palestinian conflict.

In evaluating the correlations between Black Liberation Theology and Aryan Christianity, it's important to recognize that each framework is a unique faith system, with distinct founders and theological intricacies. With that said, the philosophical origins of each exhibit, specifically in their usage of anthropology, mythology, and politics, in order to elevate one race over another, convincing similarities that cannot be ignored. Cone exalted the Black race, villainized Whites, and encouraged "the deconstruction of everything White"[61] through Black revolution in hopes of liberating traditional Black culture and lore. Aryan Christianity, on the other hand, elevated the White race, scapegoated Jews and non-Whites, and supported a maniacal uprising intended to free the people of Jewish oppression and liberate the traditional religious and cultural identities of the *Volk*.

Even more indicting is the fact that neither system is based on biblical thought. Both Cone and the German Nazified Church ignored the Bible as a "source and norm" for deducing truth, despite the fact that they both seemed happy to reintroduce carefully selected scriptures, after their conclusions had already been drawn, in order to justify their stances. Neither of these systems, Black Liberation Theology nor Aryan Christianity, despite their strategic utilization of certain biblical proof texts, would have been able to exist, let alone thrive, without formulating within themselves theological allegiances outside the boundaries of Biblical Christianity.

For Black Liberation Theology, the primary modifier was Marxism, followed by the progressive ideas of Rudolf Bultmann and Friedrich Schleiermacher. Aryan Christianity evolved through even more diverse modifiers than Black Liberation Theology, as it added to its distorted Christian foundation pantheistic Eastern mythology. These religious modifiers acted as parasitical hitchhikers within the theological frameworks of Aryan Christianity and Black Liberation Theology, sucking out the remaining marrow of Christian belief before spreading into each infectious racist heresy. Such modifiers to Christian doctrine skewed the faiths, twisting them into something heretical and no longer recognizable as Christian.

Following in their cultist footsteps, Woke Christianity, too, relies on a modifier in order to arrive at its progressive claims about Jesus. This new modifier is known as Critical Race Theory, or CRT. As we will learn in the next chapter, Critical Race Theory is culpable for doctrinally disemboweling the modern church of its views of salvation, sin, and human suffering.

CHAPTER 4

Critical Race Theory

A Tale of Two Movements

One of the things that made the civil rights movement of the 1960s in America so powerful was that, before anything else, it was a religious movement. The denouncement of Jim Crow laws, the rejection of segregation, bans on discriminatory employment policies, and demands for fair treatment under the law were all undergirded by a strong Black church in America.

At the heart of the movement were worship, prayer, and teaching of the Word. As such, it was relatively easy for kerygmatic leaders, like Billy Graham, whom Dr. Martin Luther King Jr. once praised as having "courageously brought the Christian Gospel to bear on the question of race in all of its urgent dimensions,"[1] to join alongside civil rights leaders in their pursuit of racial equality. One would expect Critical Race Theory, if it truly builds upon the legacy of the civil rights movement as many of its adherents claim, to also be at least conscious of its own Christocentric heritage.

Instead, what we find within the legal scholarship that gave birth to CRT, while religious in its own right, is a marginalized, if not absent, view of the Christian faith. Suspiciously missing from the voluminous essays and bodies of work authored by CRT founders, with few exceptions, is any clear indication that the cross of Christ had any significant impact on their moral reasoning or legal analysis. On the contrary, what we do find is a hybrid philosophy, fully secularized yet deeply religious, carrying on in the tradition, not of the civil rights movement, but the Frankfurt School, embedded with Marxism, Gnostic tendencies, and racial superiority, borrowing Christianese in order to serve its own self-interests.

Not only was Christian thought unaccounted for during the formation of CRT; its tenets are anti-Gospel, without any redeeming value, and should be rejected by believers. Yet, despite this, as we will see, Christians, especially celebrity pastors and liberal-minded academics, have blindly introduced CRT doctrine to the church and America's theological centers. To understand how this new phenomenon gained momentum, it's important to first look at the history and dogma of Critical Race Theory.

A Cynical Gnostic

In the introduction to his tendentious 1987 book, *And We Are Not Saved*, ruminating on racism in America, the late American lawyer, civil rights activist, and progenitor of Critical Race Theory, Derrick Bell could have paid homage to any one of his copious legal cases involving desegregation, or relived his experience as the first Black tenured professor at Harvard University, but instead he opened in liturgy.

This predilection for spiritual language, witnessed in Bell's and later other Critical Theorists' writings, provides initial evidence that, more than a sociological construct, Critical Race Theory is best classified as a religion. In this instance, the passage chosen by Bell was Jeremiah 8:20. The full verse, "The harvest is past, the summer has ended, and we are not saved,"[2] provided the inspiration for the title of Bell's book, which echoed the lament of "the progeny of America's slaves,"[3] who had hoped that they would be free by "the centennial of the Emancipation Proclamation," but instead witnessed, what he called, "America's continuing commitment to White domination."

Immediately, what we find concealed within the introduction to Bell's work are a framework of alienation and oppression, and an eschatology yearning for the enlightenment of the world. Bell, as it seems, is a cynical Gnostic.

This is why it was so important to first lay a historical foundation of the elemental philosophies that were forged together in recent history to form Critical Race Theory. Only by understanding Hegel's use of the dialectic, the Marxist doctrine of the proletariat (oppressed) and the bourgeoisie (oppressor), the revisionist history offered by Jesus's biographers, and Cone's invention of Black Liberation Theology is one able to fully unpack the complex elements that assemble to form CRT.

What Is Critical Race Theory?

Although it would be Kimberlé Crenshaw, a disciple of Bell's, who would eventually coin the term "Critical Race Theory," Bell pioneered the national discourse around race and legal theory as early as 1970. For Bell, the problem of suffering and disparity in the world, was easily explained as an issue of race.

> Throughout America's history, racial issues have been high among, if not central to, the country's most important concerns. Often—as when the Constitution was written, during the Civil War and Reconstruction, and throughout the decades of the civil rights movement since the Supreme Court's *Brown* decision in 1954—racial issues have riveted attention.[4]

A historical revisionist, Bell held the dispirited view that racism in America was permanently imbedded within the social and legal framework of the country and that racial progress was "largely a mirage."[5] While later Critical Race Theorists shared Bell's dismal belief in the permanence of racism, his methods for addressing societal injustices, which were more rooted in legal arguments, were upgraded to include a focus on implicit bias, microaggressions, and hate speech.

Leading the conversation as CRT fortified its tenets were Black feminists, such as Patricia Hill Collins and Audre Lorde, as well as modern literary rock stars, such as Ibram Kendi and Robin DiAngelo. Though it would take several decades, the ideology of Critical Race Theory eventually hardened into a creed-like set of beliefs that are the driving force behind CRT to this day.

But before we break this down further let's look at the basic tenets of CRT.

Critical Race Theory holds to:

- **Race as a Social Construct.** American society as we know it was created to reinforce White privilege.
- **Ethnic Gnosticism/Neo-Marxism.** Within society, people are divided solely based on race. Within American society, Whites are pitted against non-Whites.
- **The Permanence of Racism.** Without massive upheaval of our society's framework, racism will always exist.
- **Systemic Racism.** Racist ideology exists within every aspect of the structural framework of society (i.e., education, legal system, workforce)
- **Interest Convergence.** Whites will tolerate, or even encourage, the advancement of People of Color only for their own self-interest.
- **White Privilege.** Whites are born with unearned privilege that is unavailable to People of Color. In order for society to

move forward, Whites must recognize and repent of their privilege.

- **Equity over Equality.** While the words sound similar, CRT denounces equality (equal opportunity under the law) in favor of mandated government equity (equal outcomes) in an attempt to remove all economic and societal disparity.
- **Race Essentialism/Superiority.** Promotes neo-segregation and racial prejudice.
- **A Rejection of Liberalism.** CRT rejects traditional liberal beliefs, such as meritocracy, equality, legal neutrality, and colorblindness.

Theologian and church historian Carl Trueman, in his essay "Evangelicals and Race Theory," explains how these beliefs combine to take on a religious creed-like element that drives the behavior, allegiances, and activism of disciples of CRT.

Trueman draws special attention to CRT activists' "prescribed actions," and notes them as a form of worship, including raising the fist and taking the knee. Trueman also draws a similar correlation between a CRT activist's use of "orthodox words," such as "White privilege" and "systemic racism." Also present, Trueman adds, are heretical terms that, when used, "deviate from the forms" of the faith, like "non-racist" and "all lives matter."[6]

As a religious form, Trueman demonstrates, CRT is far from inviting. Through the use of manipulative, cult-like spiritual reasoning, CRT places adherents in a corner: either authenticate allegiance by confessing the CRT creed, or be declared a heretic.

The slogan "Silence is violence" is a potent rhetorical weapon. To fail to participate in the liturgy is to reject the antiracism the liturgy purports to represent—something only a racist would do.[7]

This rather convincing philosophical and cultural pressure makes Critical Race Theory, according to Trueman, "extremely seductive." As such, CRT is "hard to oppose, since it denies the legitimacy of arguments that call it into question." Through the use of "he-who-is-not-with-us-is-against-us rhetoric," Trueman points out, Critical Race Theorists are able to label critics, even those with only mild hesitancy, as part of the problem—even racists themselves. Here are just a few examples of how this reasoning manipulates agreement from the masses:

- "So, what, you don't think Black lives matter?"
- "You're against antiracism? Doesn't that make you a racist?"
- "You only say that because of your White privilege."
- "If you were really not a racist, then you would take a knee in protest."
- "Only a racist would reject the tenets of CRT."
- "By not posting on social media that Black lives matter, you're exposing your bias."

This is exactly the trap that many leading evangelicals fell into during the summer of 2020. Unprepared for the onslaught of labyrinthine arguments posited by progressives, pastors—most of whom had hardly ever heard of Critical Race Theory at that time—were pressured by their social followers to post the seemingly innocuous black square and demanded to know where they stood in support of Black Lives Matter (BLM), a Marxist and antifamily organization designed to push Critical Race Theory. Post the square and say, "Black lives matter," or be exposed as racist—these were the only two options.

To the glee of Critical Race Theorists everywhere, dozens of celebrity pastors, including Judah Smith, Carl Lentz, Craig Groeschel, T. D. Jakes, Beth Moore, and Steve Furtick, digitally bowed to the Woke mob and signified their support by posting the infamous black square. Fueled by emotional force and philosophical trickery, not to mention over one billion dollars in corporate funding,[8] it's understandable to see how many were caught off-guard. Yet, at the time of this writing, nearly two years later, not only has none of these individuals deleted their initial support of BLM, but many of them have doubled down on their advocacy.

Due to the modern complexities of the Critical Race Theory heresy, it's difficult to find precedent within church history for how to respond when such a large percentage of the church seems to have either accommodated it or bowed in support of it. But before we turn to scripture to build a proper Christian response to CRT, let's first turn our attention to the wisdom of a lesser-known third-century church bishop named Cyprian.

The Lapsed

Caecilius Cyprianus, otherwise known as St. Cyprian, was the Bishop of Carthage during one of the most turbulent eras of the early church. Forced to navigate a two-year persecution, as well as a devastating plague, Cyprian, who would eventually be beheaded for his faith, faced the challenge of restoring believers who faltered in their devotion to Christ during the Decian persecution in 250 AD. The controversy arose after the Roman emperor Decius, in an attempt to strengthen the empire, sought to impose a government-enforced religious unity in honor of pagan gods. While Decius didn't intend to target Christians through the mandate, the faithful suffered nonetheless.

The edict required every citizen to offer a sacrifice to the gods of Rome. Once complete, the sacrificer would receive a document, called a *libellus*, signed by an official, as proof of their offering. This obviously presented a problem for members of the Christian faith. The faithful were either imprisoned or killed for failure to participate, or went into hiding until the persecution was lifted. Others avoided punishment by either offering the sacrifice or bribing someone to obtain a *libellus* signed by an official even though they hadn't

completed the sacrifice themselves. Christians who offered the sacrifice were labeled *sacrificati*, and those who obtained "proof" of sacrifice by means of deceit were called *libellatici*. Once the persecution
was over, Cyprian was charged with the role of uniting the faithful
with those believers who had fallen, known as the *lapsed* or *lapsi*,
assuming they repented of their betrayal.

With great emotion and a heavy heart, Cyprian wrote of the
lapsis' hasty refusal to be counted among those who suffered for their
faith:

> They did not even wait to be arrested before going up [to
> offer sacrifice]; they did not wait to be questioned before
> they denied their faith. Many were defeated before the
> battle was joined, they collapsed without any encounter, thus
> even depriving themselves of the plea that they had sacri-
> ficed to the idols against their will. . . . Could a servant of
> God stand there and speak—and renounce Christ, whereas
> it was the world and the devil he had renounced before?[9]

Many, without confrontation or arrest, pre-emptively entered
into agreement with the mandate of Rome and offered sacrifices
to pagan gods. Those who returned to the church repentantly were
offered grace, but only after proving their devotion through what
became known as "long penance," essentially a time of testing to
ensure that their devotion to Christ was sincere. After all, this wasn't
simply a moral failure or sin of omission, but a temporary renounce-
ment of Christ and a willingness to honor a false god.

To Cyprian, this was unforgivable by man, as "only the Lord
can grant mercy."[10] Reminding the fallen believers, he adds, "Sins
committed against Him can be cancelled by Him alone who bore
our sins and suffered for us, by Him whom God delivered up for our
sins."[11] While Cyprian refused to ignore the sins of the lapsed, or
to allow them to carry on as if nothing had happened, he saved his

harshest words for his fellow clergy who abandoned their posts, in order to save their own skin:

> Gone was the devotion of bishops to the service of God, gone was the clergy's faithful integrity, gone the gener- ous compassion for the needy, gone all discipline in our behaviour. . . . Too many bishops, instead of giving encour- agement and example to others, made no account of their being God's ministers, and became ministers of earthly kings; they left their sees, abandoned their people, and toured the markets in other territories on the lookout for profitable deals. While their brethren in the church went hungry, they wanted to have money in abundance. . . . If that is what we have become, what do we not deserve for such sins, when the judgment of God warned us long since, say- ing: "If they forsake my law and walk not in my judgments: if they profane my statutes and observe not my commands: I will visit their crimes with a rod, and their transgressions with scourges"?[12]

In some ways, the departure from the faith witnessed today by Woke Christians, offering sacrifice to the gods of Critical Theory, Gnosticism, and a tyrannical state, is worse than the betrayal of the lapsed during the Decian persecution. At least at that time there was a genuine fear of death motivating the *libellatici* and *sacrificati*. But what excuse do believers have today, especially pastors, who willingly rushed to obtain their modern *libellus*, in the form of an approved black square on social media, documenting their devotion to the new Rome?

In the case of Cyprian's lapsed, many of these individuals con- fessed their sin and sought to be united back to the brotherhood of the faith, but today, the Woke refuse to even acknowledge their offense, and they not only desire to be counted among the faith- ful but are so bold as to declare that they themselves are the more devout. In such a case, how else is the church to respond other than to "expel the wicked person from among you"?[13]

Robin DiAngelo—The Neo-Colonizer

"White people in North America live in a society that is deeply separate and unequal by race, and white people are the beneficiaries of that separation and inequality,"[14] opines Robin DiAngelo as she opens her book, *White Fragility*. DiAngelo, one of the loudest voices within the field now known as CRT is a White woman herself with an extensive background in higher education with a focus on racial and social justice. In *White Fragility*, now treated as canon for Woke Christians, DiAngelo dispenses a robust argument, built upon a stout Gnostic framework, as to why all Whites are racist, privileged, and fragile. In fact, for DiAngelo, Whites are so racist that she considers it "virtually impossible" to teach a White person what racism even is; that is, unless they devote "intentional and ongoing study" to the subject, which includes buying her book or hiring her as a diversity trainer at a privileged price of $14,000 a speech.[15]

Like most Gnostics, what is difficult, or impossible for others, is easy for a guru like DiAngelo, who even though White herself, seems to understand racism with perfect precision. Part of DiAngelo's genius is in how her philosophy pads her from any outside rebuttal or debate, as anyone brave enough to disagree with DiAngelo is quickly dismissed, since he is obviously manifesting his own "white fragility" in the form of "defensiveness, argumentation . . . and other forms of pushback."[16]

But for DiAngelo, this defensiveness is necessary. As a critical social theorist, she is applying a dialectical understanding to racism, beginning first by redefining terminology. DiAngelo then abandons the original thesis (that a racist is someone who holds conscious dislike of people because of race) and, in the spirit of Hegel, then synthesizes this definition until she arrives at her preferred meaning—"racism is a system." If you're White, then you participate in the system. If you're White, then you are racist. If you are White, then you have a lot of work to do.

Interestingly, according to DiAngelo's Critical Race Theory, "People of Color may also hold prejudices and discriminate against White people, but [since] they lack the social and institutional power that transforms their prejudice and discrimination into racism," a Person of Color cannot be racist nor participate in racism.

As James Lindsay rightly points out, the beliefs of Critical Theorists, like DiAngelo, are nothing more than ethnic Gnosticism. Recall the three aspects to Gnostic ideology: alienation, an evil system, and the work or secret knowledge required to break free from it. In DiAngelo's constructed reality, although both Whites and non-Whites experience alienation (that is, that they are concretely placed within fixed roles of oppressor and oppressed), the racial alienation they may experience is a direct result of an evil system built by White authority and control. But alas, DiAngelo offers us a way out! "Do the work" to become antiracist, which includes participating in transformative learning (aka "secret knowledge") through complex diversity training.

As if ethnic Gnosticism isn't reason enough to abandon CRT, as presented, Critical Race Theory should be wholly disregarded simply on the basis of it being nothing more than a form of neo-colonization, where non-Whites are trapped in an uncivilized and savage environment, alienated, and unable to save themselves from the system of racism without the help of Whites.

Within the CRT framework, the utopian world free from systemic oppression is entirely dependent upon Whites realizing their perfection. What Critical Theorists fail to realize is that their theory inadvertently places Whites in the role of Hegel's god—an ignorant being with great potential, who created the system and holds all the power but fails to realize his greatness until he sees perfection in the people he alienated. As long as Whites do the work necessary to establish a new system free from microaggressions and institutional racism, only then can the two become one. In this sense, DiAngelo (and other CRT advocates like her) has become the Hegelian White god, finally awakened from her slumber and ready to lead People of Color toward a liberation only she can provide.

Like all Critical Theorists, Diangelo's mistake begins by denying individualism. She reasons that just as "Bill Gates's son was born into a set of opportunities that will benefit him throughout his life,"[17] Whites are born with intrinsic privilege that creates opportunities unavailable to People of Color.

Even though similar claims regarding the privilege of a Saudi prince or a child born to Beyoncé and Jay Z can be made, DiAngelo is unable to see the issue of race from any other lens than the stereotypes and wide-sweeping generalizations that her field of sociology offers. Similar to the assumptions made by Jesus's biographers about Christ, she rejects individualism, because sociology (her primary field of study) rejects individualism.

Are There Redemptive Aspects of Critical Race Theory?

Recently, I was asked by an attendee at a conference I spoke at regarding Critical Race Theory to highlight some of the redemptive aspects of CRT for Christians. The audience was likely expecting me to highlight CRT's emphasis on justice, the importance of shining light on racial inequality, and the value it serves in dismantling oppressive systems. Instead, I answered very simply, "There aren't any redemptive aspects of Critical Race Theory." As you can imagine, my answer was a shock to quite a few in the room.

Critical Race Theory is built upon a foundation of atheistic materialism, a godless ideology, completely opposed to Christianity, which holds that time, matter, and human experience form the sum total of existence. Furthermore, Christianity affirms objective, universal truth. CRT promotes varying moral standards based on the color of a person's skin, instead of God's righteous judgment. This epistemological difference is rejected outright in Proverbs 20:10 (NIV), "Differing weights and differing measures—the Lord detests them both."

Additionally, in CRT, only Whites and those in power are capable of the sin of racism, but Christianity rejects the sin of partiality based on race or socioeconomic status. For example, James instructed believers to "not show favoritism"[18] based on financial status, especially in favor of the rich, and the book of Exodus condemns mob rule and siding with someone simply because they are poor.

> Do not follow the crowd in doing wrong. When you give testimony in a lawsuit, do not pervert justice by siding with the crowd, and do not show favoritism to a poor person in a lawsuit.[19]

Biblically speaking, to receive salvation requires a total rejection of partiality, along with a heartfelt acceptance that "all have sinned and fall short of the glory of God."[20] These two beliefs remain crucial presuppositions of the Christian faith, both of which CRT denies. As such, the Bible is a proponent for equality (i.e., equal opportunity) over equity (i.e., equal outcomes). In fact, scripture goes so far as to teach that similar temptations and challenges (opportunities) face us all, yet we are all given the same grace to overcome them.

> No temptation has overtaken you except what is common to mankind. And God is faithful; he will not let you be tempted beyond what you can bear. But when you are tempted, he will also provide a way out so that you can endure it.[21]

CRT denies the commonality of the human experience and the trappings of sin, teaching that People of Color experience unique temptations and challenges, unimaginable to Whites.

Additionally, CRT asserts that Whites are born with a greater level of guilt than non-Whites, due to systemic differences that exist inherently within race. CRT further opines that Whites' history of perpetuating slavery until the nineteenth century justifies this guilt, in spite of the fact that people of all skin colors bought and owned slaves at various points in history. Contrast this belief system with scripture, which directly rejects inherited guilt:

> The one who sins is the one who will die. The child will not share the guilt of the parent, nor will the parent share the guilt of the child. The righteousness of the righteous will be credited to them, and the wickedness of the wicked will be charged against them.[22]

According to the book of Ezekiel, each person is responsible for their own transgressions and is free from any guilt of their ancestors. The Deuteronomic account confirms this as well: "Parents are not to be put to death for their children, nor children put to death for their parents; each will die for their own sin."[23] Therefore, the consensus of CRT, which accuses individuals of guilt based on biological markers, hereditary bloodlines, or any other arbitrary collective parameter, instead of individual culpability, is patently unbiblical.

Two Races

Biblically speaking, humankind congenitally belongs to Adam until one is born again in Christ. This is our default state. In this predicament, scripture uses words such as "darkened,"[24] "dead in your sins,"[25] "dead in your transgressions,"[26] "separate from Christ,"[27] "excluded from citizenship,"[28] and "without hope"[29] to describe the spiritual condition of Man. This depraved reality is common to all men, and remains, regardless of genetics, geography, education, upbringing, or even moral standing, until someone is made a "new creation in Christ." Paul writes, "Therefore, if anyone is in Christ, the new creation has come: The old has gone, the new is here!"[30] As such, Christianity, in contrast to Critical Race Theory, identifies Man, not in a plethora of various racial distinctions, nor in mere humanistic categories, such as oppressor or oppressed, but in one of two spiritual conditions, in Adam or in Christ.

For those in Christ, Paul taught "There is neither Jew nor Gentile, neither slave nor free, nor is there male and female, for you are all one in Christ Jesus."[31] While this doesn't mean that a Christian is incapable of sinning; it does mean that the shackles of sin have been broken, and that now, we who are in Christ are slaves to righteousness.[32]

John wrote in his first letter concerning this:

If we claim to have fellowship with him and yet walk in the darkness, we lie and do not live out the truth. But if we walk in the light, as he is in the light, we have fellowship with one another, and the blood of Jesus, his Son, purifies us from all sin. If we claim to be without sin, we deceive ourselves and the truth is not in us. If we confess our sins, he is faithful and just and will forgive us our sins and purify us from all unrighteousness. If we claim we have not sinned, we make him out to be a liar and his word is not in us.[33]

Here again, Wokeism finds itself in opposition to biblical Christianity. According to John, fellowship with God through Christ is what grants us access to the truth and cleanses us of our sins. For Woke Christians to attempt to place fellow believers back under the bondage of sin, by demanding additional repentance after they have been freed by faith in Christ, is to attempt to undo the work of the cross. Likewise, for a person to think that they are freed from sin, simply because they aren't part of a White heteronormative hegemony, is equally ludicrous, as only in Christ is righteousness imputed unto us.

Christ and Belial

As believers, it should be obvious by now that the teachings of CRT share no common ground or redeemable space with Christianity. For this reason, it's urgent that we guard ourselves from ideology derived from CRT. Remember what Paul said:

> For what do righteousness and wickedness have in common? Or what fellowship can light have with darkness? What harmony is there between Christ and Belial? . . . What agreement is there between the temple of God and idols?"[34]

As Paul articulated, light and darkness have nothing in common; therefore, we cannot allow the evils of CRT to contaminate our faith by blending the two.

While there is still opportunity to protect our personal faith, unfortunately, as we will see, many of our Christian institutions and foundations have already allowed CRT in various forms to infiltrate their faculty, student body, and board of directors. In perfectly timed irony, even as I wrote this, a friend in Christian higher education reached out to ask if I would pray for her. When I inquired why, she informed me that her department has recently embraced CRT and was drifting away from its Christian mission. To make matters worse, this is not the first message I have received from others in similar positions. If we are to protect our long-standing Christian institutions from the influence of progressive operatives, especially those who fallaciously project themselves to be orthodox, then we must expose their corrupt tactics and deceptive ways.

CHAPTER 5

The School of Woke

The Secularization of America's Christian Institutions

"Let every student be plainly instructed, and earnestly pressed to consider well, the maine end of his life and studies is, to know God and Jesus Christ,"[1] stated the 1646 "Rules and Precepts" of Harvard University. Like nearly all Western universities at the time, Harvard was founded with one purpose in mind: to train up the next generation of clergy. Founded in New England in 1636 on the coattails of the Protestant Reformation, Harvard was uniquely placed in the balance of social order and ecclesiastical authority. Rooted in Puritanical thought, Harvard, according to George M. Marsden, author of *The Soul of the American University Revisited*, was "governed by a board of overseers, or trustees, made up equally of clergy and magistrates."[2] Thus, the college was positioned, as neither State nor Church, to exist in the brackish waters between the two, holding each accountable to the Christian faith and Western values.

Harvard students were expected to discipline themselves to read the scriptures at least twice a day since "the word giveth light" and "understanding to the simple."[3] As a college founded upon the motto *Veritas pro Christo et Ecclesia*,[4] translated to "Truth for Christ and Church," the founders of Harvard believed that as students grew in their understanding of spiritual truths, it would enhance their observations of language, logic, and other practical learning.[5] Additionally, students were asked to refrain from any profanity and from taking God's name in vain, so that they weren't given over to, as the Apostle Paul wrote, a "reprobate mind."[6] Students believed to have breached any of the school rules, or who were found in violation of scriptural values were admonished and, if necessary, disciplined and dismissed.

Today, nearly 400 years later, this very same university just hired its newest president to the chaplaincy—an atheist named Greg Epstein. Epstein oversees the school's 40 chaplains of various faiths and defended his placement despite his lack of faith saying, "There is a rising group of people who no longer identify with any religious tradition but still experience a real need for conversation and support around what it means to be a good human."[7]

Likely a Harvard that its namesake and patron Pastor John Harvard would neither recognize nor approve of, the school today has drifted from a pinnacle of religious training, to a humanistic hotbed of progressive ideology. To illustrate this, I recently participated in an official Harvard "historical" tour of the campus offered by the school's information office. For an hour, our guide (a male graduate student with multicolored painted fingernails) showed us around the beautiful campus without a single mention of the college's religious beginnings, nor did we visit one of the school's three chapels. Instead, what we were presented with was report after report of Harvard's errors in diversity, its later efforts in inclusion, as well as several apologies for its failure to integrate more diverse policies sooner. Also discussed was its first female president, its large secular stained-glass collection, the school's grievances with George Washington, and how the campus honors all religions equally. While some may wonder whether this is just the result of a liberal tour guide gone rogue, I'll note that absent from Harvard's website is also any mention of its faith heritage. The point is perhaps made the clearest, though, by Harvard's revised motto, which has been shortened, removing both "Christ" and "Church," in perfect irony, leaving only *Veritas*.

Similar stories could be told about Yale, Princeton, Notre Dame, and even the University of Michigan, which was once known for being very supportive and sympathetic to Christian teaching.[8] All have degenerated from their religious roots and embraced postmodern ideals, such as Critical Theory, universalism,[9] and atheism.

There are many reasons why the faith foundations of America's Ivy League and landmark universities eroded. Marsden cites the popularity of Darwinism,[10] the influence of Immanuel Kant and Georg Hegel's[11] critical theories, and the rise of Unitarianism,[12] an early form of Progressive Christianity that denied the Trinity and upheld the Historical Jesus, among American clergy. In most of these cases, though, the shift from spiritual to secular took place gradually over the past several hundred years. Today, secularism is so ingrained within the modern ethos of these historic universities, that hardly anyone would be surprised at their lack of preference and, in many cases, disdain for Christianity. In fact, more shocking are the isolated stories that surface occasionally wherein the universities present studies or findings that offer support for biblical truth, such as in the realm of archeology[13] or in quantum mechanics.[14]

The reason that at least a superficial awareness of the process of secularization within American universities is so necessary to our conversation about Woke Christianity is that the process is repeating itself today, not among Ivy League institutions but within second-generation Christian higher education in schools like Biola University, Azusa Pacific University, Seattle Pacific University, and Wheaton College. These institutions, most of which were founded in the late 1800s to early 1900s, became necessary as America's more historic universities began sliding into progressive thought.

This shift required denominations to re-establish theological centers focused on biblical truth and the cultivation of more evangelical pastors and missionaries. Yet today, these universities are facing
the exact same drift toward secularization, risking the loss of the
few remaining trusted voices in American higher education. But
unlike schools founded 400 years prior, these institutions may have
a chance of being redeemed, that is if Christians can break through
their apathetic tendencies in order to make their voices heard.

Going Woke

As his brush carefully caressed the brick façade alongside the east wall
of Bardwell Hall, Los Angeles artist Kent Twitchell likely remained
oblivious to the 30-year controversy his skilled strokes would ignite.
Painted in 1989, "The Word," better known as the "Jesus Mural," is a
nearly 40-foot-tall portrait of an olive-skinned and compassionate-
looking Christ with eyes gazing into the heavens, draped by a
robe and red sash, with a large Bible in His grasp. The work was
commissioned by Biola, a private Christian University outside Los
Angeles. Twitchell's depiction of Christ, located on the side of a
science building on Biola's campus, has been at the intersection of
an interminable protest accusing the work, which is valued at over
$300,000,[15] of historical inaccuracy, being a "graven image,"[16] and
even supporting "institutionalized racism."[17]

"The intent of those who find the mural overbearing and repressive is not to make a political point,"[18] consoled Barry Corey, president of Biola. Corey, who has been at the center of much of the debate
surrounding the mural, originally made the decision to restore the
work in 2010 but later seemed to regret his decision in a subsequent
public letter repenting for not doing so with more consideration of
the sorrow and anguish caused by the painting, confessing, "that this
mural—despite its noble intention—is an image of alienation."[19]

While one may expect such division over the Messiah at a
secular college, Biola is one of the most pre-eminent faith-based

universities in the country. How could this happen? Like many of its higher-education Christian counterparts, Biola is feeling the pressure to stay relevant in the realm of diversity, equity, and inclusion. While there was a time when diversity programs assisted underprivileged students in need, such as low-income students or English-as-a-new-language students, many of these programs, funded by state and local grants, have now become overrun by Woke doctrines and policies driven by critical race ideologies.

The temptation exists, as we hear of accounts such as the Jesus Mural, to pinpoint our frustration at a single institution, like Biola. But in light of the systemic national shift present within faith communities toward CRT, participating in isolated accusations feels no longer tenable. If Christianity in America is to survive, it will require reclaiming the fallen institutions that formerly served as sound guides for America's current and future clergy . . . but this might be easier said than done.

Christian in Name Only

An hour north of Biola University sits another well-known school, Azusa Pacific University (APU). According to its "What We Believe" page, APU is an "evangelical Christian university" that "affirms the supremacy of Christ in all areas of life."[20] Despite its so-called statement of faith, over the last several years Azusa has made national headlines for Woke policies related to race and sexuality.

For example, in 2020, an APU professor, writing to author and journalist Rod Dreher, blew the whistle on the school's provost and diversity officers for pushing onto students politically charged Left-leaning resources that promote CRT and other anti-biblical ideas.[21] The list includes a link to the debunked 1619 Project, as well as resources from dozens of conspicuous Critical Theorists, such as Ibram Kendi, Kimberlé Crenshaw, Audre Lorde, Patricia Hill Collins, and Robin Diangelo.[22]

The professor, writing to Dreher[23] regarding the list, offered:

Faculty are encouraged "to make a monthly commitment to read, watch, or listen to one of the resources" shared via a link which has also been provided to our students. You'll notice that the resources were not compiled by our faculty but by one of our many offices for diversity (can't have too many). I have hardly investigated all of them, but from what I can tell, few, if any, of the resources, pretend to have any kind of biblical approach to racial reconciliation, and many are outright hostile to the clear, orthodox teaching of scripture.

Shouldn't a prerequisite of a "Christian college" be a commitment to a Christian worldview? Rather than encouraging students to immerse themselves in the scriptures, which deal robustly with pertinent issues, such as forgiveness, mercy, and justice, the Woke leadership at APU thought it better to push materials written by atheists, Marxists, and racists. For Christian faculty, charged with training up the next generation of Christian thinkers, this behavior is nothing short of reprehensible.

Prayer and Protest

With arms linked in religious solidarity, approximately 200 students at APU gathered in 2018 in protest against the Christian school's ban of LGBTQ relationships between students. Offering support, a seminary professor at the school, Rob Muthiah, applauded the students' display, calling it, "consistent with . . . Christ's message of love."[24] The university, once known for its Wesleyan holiness theology and alumni, like Christian leadership guru John Maxwell and conservative pastor John MacArthur, ultimately reversed its decision to uphold the policy in favor of the progressive student mob.

Distancing the school even further from its once orthodox position, the following year, APU chaplain Dr. Kevin Mannoia praised California bill ACR 99, which "calls upon religious leaders to counsel on LGBTQ matters from a place of love, compassion and knowledge of the psychological and other harms of conversion therapy."[25] Unethical versions of conversion therapy, like electric shock,[26] have been used in the past and created a need for bans on certain practices. But those are already illegal in California. The term "conversion therapy" has been broadened under the proposed resolution to cover any attempt to "change sexual orientation," which could arguably include Christian evangelism or any call to submit to biblical truth.

Dr. Michael Brown, author and the host of the *Line of Fire* radio program, has been outspoken against ACR 99 and once asked on his program, "Who gave the government the right to issue a call like this? Who gave the government the right to tell religious leaders that they cannot help people with unwanted same-sex attractions pursue change?"[27] As Brown points out, the resolution, which is aimed at silencing Christian influence, places liberal policy on the level of objective truth, demonstrating yet again that the Left has no real interest in the separation of Church and State but seeks a Church that is subservient to the State.

Nicole Russell, in an opinion piece for the *Washington Examiner*, captured the intent of the bill precisely. "This resolution is meant to pave the way for penalizing religious communities in California, for standing up for what they believe in, a direct violation of their First Amendment rights,"[28] she wrote. The bill, which seeks to cripple the church and normalize LGBTQ lifestyles, objectively states that alternative sexual persuasions are "not a disease, disorder, illness, deficiency or shortcoming" but rather "natural variations that occur in sexual orientation and gender identity." Starting from this false premise that sexual variations are normal and not the result of abuse, sin, or disobedience, the bill targets pastors, Christian counselors, churches, and Christian universities that might disagree biblically with this premise. However, biblically speaking, this position isn't viable.

Christian advocates of the bill often point to the fact that the word "homosexual" didn't appear in English translations of the New Testament until 1946, implying that the church's view of homosexuality as a sin is only a modern invention and should thus be discarded. At the center of the debate is an obscure compound Greek word invented by Paul, *arsenokoitai*, which translates to "men who bed with other men."[29] Whereas orthodox Christians view this term, which is used in both 1 Corinthians 6:9 and 1 Timothy 1:10, as pertaining to all homosexual acts, Progressive Christians have advocated that the term only condemns male prostitutes and not homosexuality in general.

Kevin DeYoung, a systematic theology professor and author of the book *What Does the Bible Really Teach About Homosexuality?* directly addressed the controversy surrounding *arsenokoitai*.

> Paul is quite deliberately pulling from the Torah to make this new word. So he has in his mind all that was written in the Old Testament. And that's part of the reason why we can't just say, "Well Leviticus has a lot of strange things and so we shouldn't pay attention to Leviticus." Because Paul is explicitly drawing this teaching into the New Testament to coin this word which, given the context in Leviticus and how it's used elsewhere after the New Testament, means men having sex with other men. And there is no real other interpretation.[30]

The passage DeYoung is referring to in Leviticus reads: "Do not have sexual relations with a man as one does with a woman; that is detestable."[31] The New Testament adds further rebukes,[32] such as Paul's own words in Romans:

> Because of this, God gave them over to shameful lusts. Even their women exchanged natural sexual relations for unnatural ones. In the same way the men also abandoned natural relations with women and were inflamed with lust for one another. Men committed shameful acts with other men, and received in themselves the due penalty for their error.[33]

Contrary to resolutions like ACR 99, the Bible is clear: Perversions of gender and sexuality are clearly recognized as sin by God. So the question is, why are so many Christian institutions unwilling to align themselves with a biblically ordained framework for sexual purity?

For instance, in early 2021, the faculty senate at Seattle Pacific University (SPU), another private Christian school, issued a vote of "no confidence" in the board of directors over the school's adherence to hiring policies that supported a biblical view of sexuality and gender. The vote, which was backed by 70 percent of the faculty, came on the heels of a lawsuit against the university filed by Jéaux Rinedahl, an adjunct nursing professor who was allegedly denied a full-time position due to his sexual orientation. Kevin Neuhouser, a sociology professor and faculty adviser for an LGBTQ student group on SPU's campus said, "Right now the board is the last remaining group that has not yet come to recognize that LGBTQ individuals can be faithful Christians, and as faculty and staff they would play positive roles on our campus, if we can hire them."[34]

What's most concerning in each of these instances is that the pressure within to abandon biblical precepts doesn't appear to be coming from groups outside of the school, but rather originates internally through students, staff, and school chaplains who hold progressive ideology. If these occurrences were only driven by a few select liberal-minded students who perhaps came to the university for nonreligious reasons, it would be more understandable. But the fact that the university is allowing paid faculty to participate in steering the institutions away from their mission, or even worse, that the individuals charged with protecting the religious mission of the universities (the chaplains themselves) are serving as co-conspirators in the voyage away from scripture toward more progressive shores, either demonstrates the administrators' complete incompetence to lead or shows that the administrations themselves have been infiltrated sufficiently by Leftist actors with malicious intent.

After witnessing such egregious inconsistencies among doctrinal confession, hiring practices, and institutions' adopted social policies, it's natural to wonder why these shifts are taking place. Is the apparent national synchronization of schools changing their stance on doctrinal issues mere coincidence? Is it just a natural progression of culture? Are there contributing factors present within the church itself? Or is there something more sinister afoot?

Follow the Money

First published in 1958, W. Cleon Skousen's *The Naked Communist* expertly exposes the patient strategies of Communism to remake the Western world. Mostly notably, the book contains a detailed list of the 45 goals of Communism.[35] This same list, gathered by U.S. intelligence, was presented to Congress in 1963 by then Florida Representative Albert S. Herlong Jr. (D). It offers a chilling understanding of just how insidious and farsighted the Communist agenda in America is. While the list has been republished in countless forms throughout the years, two of the goals it contains are critical to understanding what's happening in Christian institutions:

> **Rule #17.** Get Control of the Schools. Use them as transmission belts for socialism and current Communist propaganda. Soften the curriculum. Get control of teachers' associations. Put the party line in textbooks.[36]

> **Rule #27.** Infiltrate the churches and replace revealed religion with "social" religion. Discredit the Bible and emphasize the need for intellectual maturity which does not need a "religious" crutch.[37]

Skousen reveals that Communists planned to accomplish these goals in the schools through placing Socialists and Communists in the classroom. The goal was to rewrite history, discredit historical heroes, like Christopher Columbus or Thomas Jefferson, and mold a "detached and illiterate citizenry that is malleable to a false narrative."[38] Within Christian organizations, the strategy is similar, as the church is invaded through pseudo-Christian organizations run by Leftists masquerading as Christ-followers. Fueled by dark money, these groups infiltrate orthodox religious communities, through content creation, activism, and persuasive donations all intended to erode existing spiritual foundations in favor of Marxist ideology over time.

For those unaware of the existence of dark money within Christian institutions and nonprofits, this might come as a shock, but essentially, it's a shell game. Leftist billionaires funnel money through their foundations to either pop-up organizations or to existing conservative institutions. Pop-ups are used for messaging and reprogramming conservatives to see Leftist ideas as more biblical.

An example of this would be the Evangelical Immigration Table (EIT), tied to George Soros money,[40] which was used to support open borders and mass migration initiatives. Activities such as these are often presented as "being the hands and feet of Jesus," when in reality, they are clandestine activities set forth to demolish democracy and re-envision America into a more progressive state, free from a Judeo-Christian framework. Essentially, it's a plot to use the church itself to de-Christianize the country.

Within Christian institutions such activities follow a similar pattern. Donations are made to a university, usually directed by a progressive billionaire or his foundation. At first, these donations, which are often quite sizable, may be presented as a write-off with no strings attached. But over time, repeat donations are made with increasing stipulations.

Michael O'Fallon, the founder and CEO of Sovereign Alliance, explained to me the process he's witnessed firsthand:

So the giant checks start to get written. It starts off this way. And I can say this personally, because I was on the board of an organization that did this. It starts off with a major financial donation. . . . And then the next year, "Well, we would like to give more, but there's some things that we would like for you to consider. . . ." And then it goes from "consider" to, "we need you to do." . . . And now you're being asked to go to others, to encourage them to do the same thing. So you start having that conversation, "Hey, there's a change that's happening. There's nothing you can do about [it]. You need to be on this side if you want things to go well. If you're on that side over there, things aren't going to go well for you and don't oppose us. But I'm telling you where we need to go with things is more focused on social justice. . . ." Which is the same thing that Soros has been doing for years. And if you've ever read *The Alchemy of Finance*, you understand that it's the same process of transitioning the faith into something that is not focused on individual salvation or even corporate salvation, but it's more focused upon societal change.[41]

Soros, who was declared "The Man Who Moves Markets" by Bloomberg,[42] is known for influencing global economies and social policies through his wealth. Soros's book, *The Alchemy of Finance*, is his attempt to explain his economic theory of reflexivity. Soros believes that investor perceptions and economic fundamentals (real data) exist in a sort of loop, directly impacting one another, independent of any objective reality or truth. While Soros is known for his use of reflexivity in manipulating markets, he also believes the principle applies to "all social phenomena" and is capable of introducing "a new morality."[43] In the epilogue, Soros wrote:

I was surprised to find an avid interest in the concept of reflexivity. As I have noted in the book [*The Alchemy of Finance*], reflexivity could also be described as a kind of dialectics. . . . It is exactly these connotations that make the concept so fascinating for the Chinese because it allows them to modify Marxist ideology without breaking with it. Hegel propounded a dialectic of ideas; Marx turned the idea on its head and espoused dialectical materialism; now there is a new dialectic that connects the participants' thinking with the events in which they participate—that is, it operates between ideas and material conditions. If Hegel's concept was the thesis and Marxism the antithesis, reflexivity is the synthesis. . . . Thus, the concept of reflexivity leads directly to the concept of an open society.[44]

As O'Fallon reveals, leftist billionaires, like Soros, use their money to transform not just the Western world but morality itself. Jesus, of course, stands in the way of this, so a dialectic of reflexivity is applied, gradually changing the church's mind regarding the nature and person of Christ.

Consider Biola University's well-documented relationship with Chinese Indonesian billionaire James Riady. Riady, who considers himself a reformed Christian,[45] was convicted of violating U.S. campaign finance laws for donating foreign money to the Democratic Party during the Clinton years.[46] His son, Henry, who lives in Indonesia, is a graduate of Biola University and was added to its board in 2015.[47] During his tenure on the board, according to ClarionProject.org (a watchdog organization that tracks foreign funding to American universities), two of Riady's companies donated large gifts to Biola University.[48]

Similar donations have been made to the school from the Bahamas-based Templeton Religion Trust,[49] which serves to carry out the late Sir John Templeton's progressive wishes in regard to religion. Templeton who was known as an "open-minded"[50] Presbyterian who downplayed the authority of scripture, ironically served on the board for the American Bible Society during his lifetime. Providing a glimpse into his theology, Templeton.org states:

Declaring that relatively little is known about the divine through scripture and present-day theology, [Templeton] predicted that "scientific revelations may be a gold mine for revitalizing religion in the 21st century."[51]

As such, Templeton's foundation seems committed to furthering his goal of "revitalizing religion," which appears to be progressive code for "redefining religion," through key investments into influential Christian institutions. To what degree donations from Templeton or Riady come with strings attached, only those receiving them can know for sure, but what is clear is that as the money flows in, Christian institutions are transforming—and at a rapid pace. But these tactics aren't just being used within higher education; dark money is also changing how Americans think about the environment.

Creation Care

Adorning the header of the "Evangelical Declaration on the Care of Creation,"[52] issued by the Evangelical Environmental Network (EEN) (a decoy Right-wing organization that promotes Leftist environmental policies to evangelicals), is Psalm 24:1: "The Earth is the Lord's, and the fulness thereof." According to Hayden Ludwig, Senior Investigative Researcher at Capital Research Center, the EEN is funded by major Left-leaning donors, such as the Rockefeller Brothers Fund, the Hewlett Foundation, and even the infamous Clinton Foundation.[53] While targeting Christians, the language of the declaration feels more pagan in nature, with references to God as "Sacred Spirit," and our planet as "Sacred Earth." Ludwig shared that the initial goal of campaigns such as these is to "rebrand global warming"[54] in such a way to make the issue seem more serious to conservatives and evangelicals. "Green preaching," Ludwig reveals, is only phase one of the plan, though.

If the campaign succeeded, creation care would create a huge, bipartisan coalition of Christians and center-left environmentalists (who would presumably see through the rebranding) eager for climate change action. If it was *wildly* successful, it would break evangelicals off from the Republican Party—perhaps permanently. The stakes couldn't be higher.[55]

The declaration itself, written in an attempt to convince evangelicals to embrace the existence of global warming, states:

We call on all Christians to work for godly, just, and sustainable economies which reflect God's sovereign economy and enable men, women and children to flourish along with all the diversity of creation. We recognize that poverty forces people to degrade creation in order to survive; therefore we support the development of just, free economies which empower the poor and create abundance without diminishing creation's bounty. . . . I ask You, Sacred Spirit, to inspire people of faith like me to hold the United States government—especially the EPA—responsible for allowing businesses and corporations to pollute our waterways. All Americans should have access to clean drinking water. As we watch sea levels rise, help us to have the courage to demand protection for wetlands that protect our homes and communities from flooding. We must be your hands and feet, caring for this Sacred Earth which we share with all living beings.[56]

The Left's attempt to transform the evangelical view of the environment is likely, among other things, a strategic play to reinforce globalism. After all, it's the responsibility of the world, not just one isolated country, to care for the environment. In the Left's pursuit of a one-world utopian government, a strong sense of national sovereignty stands in the way. While much is being done at home to weaken our nation's sovereign borders, Wokeism must also exert an effort to diminish national sovereignty abroad. The problem is, one group impedes this effort—Israel. As such, the Christian Left is doing its part to change American's opinion of the Holy Land.

Anti-Israel Sentiments Rising Among Woke Christians

One group leading the charge in reframing Woke Christians' relationship with Israel is Telos Group, a Washington, D.C.–based pro-Palestine nonprofit that, according to the NGO Monitor, has received over half of its funding from George Soros's Open Society Foundations.[57] "Telos," according to Charles McCracken, a writer for *Israel My Glory* magazine, "is skillfully framed with emotional snapshots and sound bites for the evangelical audience, and the itinerary is carefully controlled to maximize the impact of a one-sided message that Palestinian-Arabs are the so-called victims of Israeli oppression."[58]

Speaking of what he believes is Telos Group's hidden agenda against Israel, Christian media analyst for the Committee for Accuracy in Middle East Reporting in America (CAMERA) Dexter Van Zile warns that the nonprofit provides "Palestinian leaders access to influentials in the Evangelical community that they would not otherwise have. These influentials then lend their credibility to the anti-Zionist cause."[59]

These influential individuals include: *Relevant* magazine publisher Cameron Strang, who attended a Telos pilgrimage to Palestine;[60] Christian writer and CEO of Storybrand Donald Miller, who also served on President Barack Obama's Presidential Advisory Council on Fatherhood and Healthy Families;[61] and Lynne Hybels, wife of Bill Hybels, the former senior pastor of Willow Creek Community Church, who served on the Telos Presidential Advisory Council. Each individual has arguably used their platform to tell partial narratives of the Israel–Palestine conflict and redefine what justice looks like in the region, while simultaneously downplaying traditional Christian views that stand in support of Israel.

As Wokeism continues to expand, it's expected to see a trend where automatic support for Israel wanes. *The Christian Century* reported in as early as 2014 that an increase in pro-Palestinian sentiments in progressive churches has caused some mainstream churches to divest funds and boycott goods made in the Holy Land, "because of its occupation of the Palestinian territories."[62]

The Almighty Dollar

Leftists continue to demonstrate that there is no end in sight as to how far they will go to demolish Christian institutions, rewrite traditional beliefs, and even disrupt long-standing American foreign relations. Fueled by dark money and instituted by backroom deals between Woke operatives, the agenda of the Left is rapidly deteriorating once-strong organizations and turning them into hives for progressive politics. While these issues should be concerning, the Left has found a new weapon to fuel Woke ideology, and the church is buying into it: public health.

CHAPTER 6

Parishes and Plagues

The Church Has Failed

"As Christians, we have failed to follow biblical mandates, failed to honor and respect others and failed to authentically embody the love of Jesus Christ,"[1] writes Reverend David Wilson Rogers for an article that appeared at the top of Yahoo News. Rogers, the pastor of First Christian Church in Carlsbad, New Mexico, also made waves in 2014 after coming out alongside the Indianapolis-based Disciples LGBTQ Alliance in support of same-sex marriage.[2] In what appears to be crafted by an ecclesiastic of great devotion to Christian orthodoxy, Rogers writes:

> The root of the failure is idolatry. An idol in Scripture is anything that becomes the focus of worship, attention and dedication which is not God. Although idolatry is nothing new in Christianity, the perverse distortions of the Christian faith that have permeated so much of our American culture are a huge part of the problem as to why Christianity has so

miserably failed. Rather than trusting in Jesus Christ, far too many Christians have placed their ultimate trust in partisan politics. Worse yet, the reality of COVID-19 was quickly weaponized by both extremes of the partisan ideological divide. Rather than seeing the global pandemic as a public health crisis, it quickly was used to define partisan platforms, partisan belief systems and fidelity to partisan ideals.

In case the irony isn't obvious, Rogers, who proudly abandoned all biblical orthodoxy in regard to gender and sexuality to support sinful sexual practices, is complaining of the "perverse distortions of the Christian faith" found in those unwilling to wear a mask, shelter in place, or take the jab[3]—none of which is directly addressed in scripture (we'll talk more about that shortly).

The article, of course, makes no mention of Rogers's heretical position on marriage, giving zero indication to the casual reader that this "Reverend" is anything less than a bipartisan lover of God and expert on biblical authority rather than a left-wing activist and Progressive Christian.

The most important aspect to note of Rogers's article, though, is the phrase "public health crisis." According to Michael O'Fallon, public health is the chink in the armor of constitutional rights that Leftist operatives seek to exploit. In a series of tweets, O'Fallon divulged that the director of the Centers for Disease Control and Prevention (CDC), Rochelle Walensky, was a faculty member of the T.H. Chan School of Public Health at Harvard University. The T.H. Chan School of Public Health, named for the father of two influential Hong Kong billionaires, is what, in the opinion of O'Fallon, "brought alchemic, autocratic, technocratic 'public health' policy to the United States."[5]

By applying George Soros's theory of reflexivity discussed in the previous chapter, public opinion in America shifted to view the collective needs of public health as of greater importance than constitutional rights. This dialectical change allowed the Biden administration, as well as power-hungry state governors, to abuse emergency powers in order to enact wide-sweeping tyrannical restrictions, such as lockdowns, quarantines, mask mandates, and school closures. While some resistance was mustered, consisting mostly of outspoken Republicans and Conservatives, large majorities either complied or remained silent.

This Marxist transformation of America couldn't have been accomplished, though, simply through government mandate or even political propaganda. Just as the Third Reich found a convincing ally in the Nazified German Church, this new repressive American regime required a respected partner to authenticate the COVID-19–born "public health crisis" and verify the necessity of laying down individual rights for the good of the collective. Perfectly crafted for the job, Progressive Christianity in America understood the assignment and stepped into the role.

Are You Pro-Life?

"Jesus reminds us that the two greatest commandments are to love God and love our neighbor. Submitting to our government honors God. Following the stay-at-home order and practicing social distancing to help slow the spread is loving our neighbor,"[6] wrote Richard Nelson, director of the Commonwealth Policy Center, in an open letter to churches throughout Kentucky. In the letter, which wrongly criticized pastors for "resisting the government's stay at home orders,"[7] Nelson affirmed that governmental compliance in regard to COVID-19 is the only "pro-life position."

Pro-Choice America, an abortion advocacy group, employed nearly identical language in a recent document it released called "Pro-Life Hyprocrisy on COVID-19." In it, it too accused Conservatives of not valuing people's lives, by ignoring the "threat of the virus" and of failing "to work towards solutions that could protect public health."[8] The document, which contains 70 pages of Marxist-like propaganda, denigrates politicians, such as South Dakota Governor

Kristi Noem and Florida Governor Ron DeSantis, as well as conservative talk show hosts like Glenn Beck, calling them "extremists" for promoting constitutional freedoms and personal responsibility over public health issues.

"It is important for us to remember that the church never actually closed, just the doors to our buildings," states another document provided to churches by the Humanitarian Disaster Institute at Wheaton College. It further encouraged churches to maintain social distancing, limit in-person gathering, and remained masked. One of the reference guide's creators, Kent Annan, a Woke Christian who also recently authored a pro-globalization article for *Christianity Today*, focused on the inequity of the COVID-19 vaccine, in which he made the case that evangelicals should be more concerned about whether they should get their third COVID booster shot, or whether they should "refuse it in protest and solidarity with people in less wealthy nations, in an attempt to pressure the U.S. and pharmaceuticals to better mobilize to provide vaccines for the rest of the world."[9]

Leftist groups, led by activists like Annan and Nelson, work hard to revise the churches understanding of the Gospel to view obedience to Romans 13 as synonymous with willingly submitting to governmental overreach. Such a viewpoint is truly spiritual abuse, using the scriptures to manipulate the masses to passively submit to any and all edicts offered by corrupt officials.

Curiously, this same precept would never apply to women who are physically, emotionally, and sexually abused by their spouses. Does scripture call them to "submit to their husband," without taking into account any of the atrocities being acted out against them? Of course not, and there isn't a pastor in the country, in their right mind, who would claim that submitting to abuse in marriage is "obedience unto the Lord." At minimum, pastors would counsel a woman to seek help, ensure that she's in a safe position, free from harm, and, only then, work with counsel to see if the marriage can be reconciled.

Obedience and Resistance

Yet, when it comes to the Christian Left, they not only recommend not fleeing from the abuse of the State, but that as Christians, we should see such instances of force, from shutting down churches, to masking our children in schools, to calls for forced vaccinations, as direct expressions of our duty to Christ that demand our full submission.

But this is not what Romans 13:1-5 (NIV), nor anything else in the Bible, calls for (emphasis added):

> Let everyone be subject to the governing authorities, for there is *no authority except that which God has established. The authorities that exist have been established by God. Consequently, whoever rebels against the authority is rebelling against what God has instituted, and those who do so will bring judgment on themselves. For rulers hold no terror for those who do right, but for those who do wrong. Do you want to be free from fear of the one in authority? Then do what is right and you will be commended. For the one in authority is God's servant for your good. But if you do wrong, be afraid, for rulers do not bear the sword for no reason. They are God's servants, agents of wrath to bring punishment on the wrongdoer. Therefore, it is necessary to submit to the authorities, not only because of possible punishment but also as a matter of conscience.*

In this passage, Paul makes it clear that true authorities, established by God, are in place in order to punish wrongdoers and protect God's people, as well as all citizens who submit themselves to their *benevolent* leadership. This passage is not describing unjust leaders, tyrants, or dictators, who applaud rioters and worship criminals, while punishing the common man. Such a government or leader has fallen from the position which God has established, becoming a terror against those who do right, and an ally for those who do wrong.

Romans 13 can't possibly apply to a truly totalitarian regime, because such a regime not only ignores God but seeks to take His place. As such, Romans 13 isn't about unquestioned obedience to the State; rather, it's about recognizing the role one plays within the context of an ordered world in a civilized society. As theologian N. T. Wright explains:

> Paul's point is not the maximalist one that whatever governments do must be right and that whatever they enact must be obeyed, but the solid if minimalist one that God wants human society to be ordered; that being Christian does not release one from the complex obligations of this order; and that one must therefore submit, at least in general, to those entrusted with enforcing this order.[10]

For Wright, this commitment to civil orders has its limitations, and at times, the church must stand up to remind the leaders, despite their ordered authority, of God's authority over them. This, though, as Wright explains, will likely not be without consequence:

> If it is true that the church is called to announce to the world that Jesus Christ is Lord, then there will be times when the world will find this distinctly uncomfortable. The powers that be will need reminding of their responsibility, more often perhaps as the Western world moves more and more into its post-Christian phase, where, even when churchgoing remains strong, it is mixed with a variety of idolatries too large to be noticed by those who hold them, and where human rulers are more likely to acknowledge the rule of this or that "force" than the rule of the creator. And if the church attempts this task of reminding, of calling the powers to account for their stewardship, it will face the same charges, and perhaps the same fate, as its Lord. It is at that

point that decisions have to be made in all earnestness, at that point that idolatry exacts its price.[11]

Instead of "calling the powers to account," the Woke Christians in America have ignored the Word of God and sided with the State. While we've acknowledged many influences that led us to this place, ultimately, the passivity and indifference toward biblical truth found within progressive faith movements is an attempt to escape persecution. Persecution, though, is part of the Christian experience, and while not directly from God, it is evidence of our obedience to Him. In fact, it is persecution that tends to usher the church into its finer hours, granting us a road map of how to live for Christ, despite the hatred and control exhibited by the world. As Paul writes in Romans 12 (NIV):

> Bless those who persecute you; bless and do not curse. . . .
> Live in harmony with one another. Do not be proud, but
> be willing to associate with people of low position. Do not
> be conceited. Do not repay anyone evil for evil. Be careful
> to do what is right in the eyes of everyone. If it is possible,
> as far as it depends on you, live at peace with everyone. Do
> not take revenge, my dear friends, but leave room for God's
> wrath, for it is written: "It is mine to avenge; I will repay,"
> says the Lord. On the contrary: "If your enemy is hungry,
> feed him; if he is thirsty, give him something to drink. In
> doing this, you will heap burning coals on his head." Do not
> be overcome by evil, but overcome evil with good.

In this beautiful and convicting passage, Paul's exhortation to the church regarding persecution and unjust treatment never calls believers to submit to such acts, but rather that in our response, we should be free from conceit, evil, and revenge. Rather than rioting and looting when we don't get our way, or seeking to harm those who are persecuting us, the church is called to overcome and resist evil through good works. This might be calmly speaking out at a school board meeting, civilly resisting government mandates, or praying for those in authority, even when they are in the wrong. No matter how we respond, though, we should not be deceived into thinking that the Christians' response should be one of passivity or quiet submission to injustice. Scripture provides no shortage of examples of people of God who understood what righteous resistance entailed, including:

- Hebrew midwives who ignored Pharaoh's edict to kill all male babies and saved Moses.[12]
- Rahab, who disobeyed the King of Jericho's command to report any spies and instead helped the Hebrew spies escape, eventually leading to a successful siege of the city.[13]
- Obadiah, who hid 100 prophets from Jezebel in order to spare their lives.[14]
- Johoiada, the priest, who led a resistance to remove Athaliah from her illegitimate rule.[15]
- Queen Vashti, who refused to objectify herself before the king and his court.[16]
- Daniel and his men, who refused to defile themselves with the king's meat.[17]
- Shadrach, Meshach, and Abednego, who refused to bow down to the golden idol.[18]
- Daniel, who refused to submit to the king's edict and was thrown into the lion's den.[19]
- The magi, who ignored Herod's request to bring him word of Christ's birth, escaping from the country a different way.[20]
- Jesus and his disciples, who picked up grain on the Sabbath, violating the Jewish law.[21]
- Peter and John, who continued to preach publicly, even after being arrested and flogged.[22]
- Paul and Silas, who were imprisoned for preaching against the customs of civil authorities, and even continued to preach the Word after being thrown into prison.[23]

John Calvin, in his massive work *The Institutes of the Christian Religion*, summed up the occasional need for civil disobedience, when he wrote: "And, indeed, how preposterous were it, in pleasing men, to incur the offense of Him for whose sake you obey men!"[24] For Calvin, to obey men at all cost, because we perceive this to be obedience to God, would be foolish if such obedience to man led us to ultimately disobey God. Continuing, he added: "We are subject to the men who rule over us, but subject only in the Lord. If they command anything against Him, let us not pay the least regard to it, nor be moved by all the dignity which they possess as magistrates."[25]

A firm theology of delegated authority, which Calvin clearly understood, and on which he arguably laid the groundwork for the church's understanding, is absolutely necessary in order to discern when submission to a dictatorial state is appropriate and when it should be resisted. To consider this further, we must turn to a man who built upon Calvin's work, Dr. Abraham Kuyper.

Theology of the Body

In 1880, at the inauguration of the Free University of the Netherlands, Dr. Abraham Kuyper,[26] a well-respected reformed theologian, delivered a public address, in which he compared the difference between State sovereignty and what he calls "Sphere sovereignty." Kuyper introduced the idea that individual realms, what he calls spheres, have boundaries of sovereign jurisdiction, in which they experience God's grace to govern and define themselves. In State sovereignty, these individual spheres (e.g., church, family, economy, science, academics) all exist under the sovereign authority of the State, what he calls Caesarism.[27]

In contrast, under Christ's sovereignty, each of these spheres has delegated jurisdiction, or an individual liberty, that allows each realm to operate in the grace given to them, as they live and move and have their being in Christ.[28] Undoubtedly, a shift transpired post-COVID, in which a global nation-state has claimed jurisdiction over realms of authority that formerly belonged to families and individuals.

When Christ is allowed supremacy, each sphere is granted delegated authority to serve the Lord within the bounds of its jurisdiction. An example of this would be a father acting as head of his household, a group of elders operating as sovereign overseers of a local church, and a president governing the affairs of a nation. Within the State sovereignty model, individual sovereignty is all but lost, swallowed up by the unlimited and unaccountable power of the State, "disposing of persons, their life, their rights, their conscience and even their faith."[29] Where once the father had the sovereign authority to lead his family, now the State strips him of his role, usurping his authority and adopting his children as property of the State.

> "Sphere Sovereignty" defending itself against "State Sovereignty"—that is the course of world history . . . thus ancient history presents to our view among all peoples the shameful spectacle that, after persevering, and sometimes heroic struggle, freedom in one's own sphere perishes, and the power of the State, turning into Caesarism, gains the upper hand.[30]

According to Kuyper, this war for the upper hand was especially problematic in the realm of science. "There is indeed a satanic danger," Kuyper shared at the inauguration, "that some will degenerate into devils of pride, and will tempt science to arrogate unto itself that which is outside of its sphere."[31] For Kuyper, this "tyranny of science"[32] was only possible while the church was in a state of spiritual decline. With a chilling prophetic voice, Kuyper said that when this decline takes place, science will be used as a "servant of the State"[33] to "dominate the people."[34] This, of course, is exactly what has happened as public health (i.e., science) is allowed to eclipse all other spheres of jurisdiction, including the church.

Within a Christ-centric system, the State utilizes its authority (beyond national defense and enforcing the law) to offer situational guidance to families, municipalities, and private organizations. Each of these entities is then free to utilize their own sphere of sovereignty, assuming that in doing so they don't break just laws of the State, to appropriate the advice of the State into their own unique situations and environments. Thus, a free society is retained, one that is built upon the supremacy of Christ, governed by the State, and freely adhered to by sovereign and dignified people. Each man is able to lead his family and make decisions about his health, finances, and movements, based on the information provided by the State and already possessed by the Word of God.

In a State-sovereignty system, individual liberties are retracted, and as such, the advice of the State ceases to be advice and becomes non-negotiable mandates. Every other sphere, as a result, loses its own jurisdictional sovereignty and is forced to make decisions without any consideration of its own wants or needs. Such a system violates God's design for man, ignores his delegated permissions given to other spheres, and strips man of his dignity to choose.

As we see in Romans 13, when spheres of sovereignty are recognized, even in the case of a pagan State, believers are called to submit to governing authorities. But when evil reigns, and a tyrannical State is allowed to flourish, believers may have no choice but to usurp the unjust powers of the State, in order to freely operate in the faith, both in conscience and in deed. Never should this righteous resistance take the form of lawlessness, violence,[35] or anarchy, but it may require refusal to comply, depending upon the extent to which tyranny manifests itself.

To navigate this successfully, especially in light of the current mandates related to the COVID-19 health crisis, a theology of conscience must be developed. To do so, we'll need to draw insight from two of Paul's most challenging teachings on conscience.

A Theology of Conscience

Despite all of its talk of inclusion and acceptance, Woke Christianity is built upon a system of legalism. While it may be soft on moral issues, Progressive Christianity is rigidly performance-based in regard to social behaviors and the total acceptance of the agenda of the Left. Perhaps nowhere is this more evident than in the Woke Church's response to the COVID-19 vaccine.

Rather than allow an individual believer to retain personal sovereignty over their body by inquiring of the Lord (and their personal doctor) on whether the vaccine was right for them, the autocratic church of the Woke sided with the tyrannical State to undo sphere sovereignty and spiritually police the taking of the vaccine. Endowed with a theology of guilt and condemnation, the Christian Left pressured the Body of Christ to bow the knee to their mandatory system of compliance through statements like:

- Loving your neighbor is getting vaccinated.
- Jesus would get vaccinated.
- Do you want people to die?
- Submit to those in authority.
- Get vaccinated—it's the right thing to do.
- Is your freedom in Christ more important than other people's health?

While some may disagree with this, it's important that we realize that the Bible doesn't specifically address the COVID-19 vaccination. It's not the Mark of the Beast, at least not yet, and if you are someone who took the vaccine, there is no condemnation for you in Christ Jesus. For some individuals, based on their medical conditions, taking the vaccine may have been appropriate and even saved their life. I'm not a medical doctor, so while I personally have valid questions about the long-term safety and efficacy of the vaccine, this is not the point of our conversation. Some Christians have erred by entering into the same behavior of the Left, operating by force, through pressuring others *not* to get the vaccination. Often they cite ingredients from fetal cells and concerns about safety, which are fair arguments. But these same Christians have often taken other previous vaccinations made from the same fetal tissue line without any hesitation. From a biblical standpoint, issues such as these are better left to personal conscience and private pastoral counsel, which is the point of this discussion.

Guilt and condemnation, as well as legalistic adherence to a man-made system of performance, should never be a Christian's *modus operandi*. Therefore, we can acknowledge that any theology that devalues man's individual jurisdiction of personal liberty is antithetical to Christian teaching. After all, the Bible emphatically proclaims, "Where the Spirit of the Lord is, there is freedom." Thus, believers should respect and honor the lawful jurisdiction of others' (delegated authority), while rejecting any attempt by others to hijack our personal liberties through unlawful authority toward us or anyone else, which is exactly what is happening through COVID-19 mandates at the hands of power-hungry politicians and public health officers.

While the Bible might not address the COVID-19 vaccine directly, it does undoubtedly explore issues of personal conscience in the face of controversial decisions. At the forefront of these topics is Paul's instructions regarding eating meat sacrificed to idols. In 1 Corinthians 8:4-13, Paul wrote:

> So then, about eating food sacrificed to idols: We know that "An idol is nothing at all in the world" and that "There is no God but one." For even if there are so-called gods, whether in heaven or on earth (as indeed there are many "gods" and many "lords"), yet for us there is but one God, the Father, from whom all things came and for whom we live; and there is but one Lord, Jesus Christ, through whom all things came and through whom we live. But not everyone possesses this knowledge. Some people are still so accustomed to idols

that when they eat sacrificial food they think of it as having been sacrificed to a god, and since their conscience is weak, it is defiled. But food does not bring us near to God; we are no worse if we do not eat, and no better if we do. Be careful, however, that the exercise of your rights does not become a stumbling block to the weak. For if someone with a weak conscience sees you, with all your knowledge, eating in an idol's temple, won't that person be emboldened to eat what is sacrificed to idols? So this weak brother or sister, for whom Christ died, is destroyed by your knowledge. When you sin against them in this way and wound their weak conscience, you sin against Christ. Therefore, if what I eat causes my brother or sister to fall into sin, I will never eat meat again, so that I will not cause them to fall.[36]

In first-century Rome, it was nearly impossible to escape the expansive influence of paganism. Weddings, funerals, and other celebrations would often take place in pagan temples or places of worship. For Christians, to be "in the world but not of the world" meant that they might frequently come into contact with pagan activities, mystic symbols, or ceremonial foods in the marketplace that had been utilized in pagan rituals. While most of these encounters could be safely avoided, the prevalence of animal sacrifice in Roman religion required Paul to help the church establish a theology of conscience regarding the issue in order to help prevent believers from falling into sin.

"An idol is nothing," Paul begins by identifying the problem, demonstrating that the conscience of the believer, not the idol, was the real issue. The same can be said about the COVID-19 vaccine. While we can have a separate conversation about the vaccine's ingredients (which differ by brand) or of the effects of an mRNA vaccine to begin with, these conversations are better left to medical professionals, holistic practitioners, and peer-reviewed studies. From a theological standpoint,[37] the greater threat to the faith is likely not the vaccine, but the violations happening to the conscience of the Christian in the name of science.

Paul addresses the detrimental effects of forcefully violating a believer's conscience in his instructions about eating meat sacrificed to idols. More than just pressuring someone to do something that he isn't comfortable with, Paul warns that such behavior could "destroy" a person, "wound their weak conscience," and cause the offender to "sin against Christ." This is why it is so important that pro-vaccine Christians resist joining with the ranks of Progressive Christians in support of vaccine mandates. Since so many believers have expressed concerns about the vaccine's ingredients, efficacy, safety, and ultimately the agenda of control seemingly behind it, less-concerned Christians should never put these individuals (whom Paul calls the "weaker brother") in a position in which they are forced to violate their conscience through mandated vaccination.[38] Some will likely take offense to the thought that they might be considered the "weaker brother" for resisting the vaccine, especially since the common sentiment of those who consciously resisted the vaccine tends to view vaccinated Christians as "sheep" or "weak" for doing whatever the government tells them to do.

I have two thoughts regarding this. First, as Christians, does not Paul admonish us when he humbly cries, "Therefore I will boast all the more gladly about my weaknesses, so that Christ's power may rest on me. That is why, for Christ's sake, I delight in weaknesses, in insults, in hardships, in persecutions, in difficulties. For when I am weak, then I am strong"?[39] As Christians, why should we ever feel ashamed of weakness, especially when that "weakness" involves a strong desire to purify ourselves, whether in spirit or in flesh, from anything that might desecrate the temple of the Holy Spirit?

Second, to those who want to boast of their own strength for not taking the vaccine or wearing a mask (i.e., that they are so much stronger than those who have taken the vaccine or who do wear a mask), would you rather have it the other way? Namely, when speaking to the "strong," Paul commands them to ensure that their strength "does not become a stumbling block to the weak," and if it does, that they should "never eat meat again," so as not to "cause [weaker brothers] to fall."

Applied to the issue of vaccinations, this would mean that if the "strong" are the unvaxxed, they would be obligated to get vaccinated, so as to not become a stumbling block for the weaker, vaccinated brothers. Biblically, these are the only two options.

Thankfully in context, Paul is clear: those who don't partake in the "liberty" of meat sacrificed to idols are the "weak," and as such, the "stronger" should never attempt to compel them to violate that conscience to consume something, whether food or any other substance, that violates their faith and relationship with Christ. In this situation, Woke Christians who truly believe in the importance of the COVID-19 vaccine and truly care for their "weaker" brothers and sisters have only one biblical position: under no circumstances should they support forced vaccination, vaccine mandates, or vaccine passports.

Nevertheless, pro-vaccine Christians, such as Reverend Kenneth B. Thomas at the Bethesda Worship and Healing Missionary Baptist Church in Jonesboro, Arkansas, still preach guilt and condemnation toward the unvaxxed with statements like: "Mask it, vax it or choose the casket. The choice is yours."[40]

Even right-wing evangelical Franklin Graham appeared to be influenced by the pressure for Christian leaders to support vaccination, claiming, "If there were vaccines available in the time of Christ, Jesus would have made reference to them and used them."[41]

Going a step further, the Arizona Faith Network, a Leftist interfaith advocacy group, rallied hundreds of faith leaders to put pressure on Arizona Governor Doug Ducey "to extend his stay-at-home order."[42] A similar push was made in 2020 in Missouri by the St. Louis Metropolitan Clergy Coalition, whose spokesperson, Bishop Elijah Hankerson, pleaded, "Let us take shelter and stay at home until the storm passes over,"[43] while Marda Loop Church in Calgary, Alberta, after finally reopening in late 2021, required guests to present proof of double vaccination before being able to attend in person. Defending his position, the Pastor John Van Sloten offered, "We have chosen to be a church that will . . . for the sake of the vulnerable . . . have a policy that people be double vaccinated to come to live services."

Whether aware or not, churches such as these are constructing a new theology, infused with a cultural Marxism that no longer cries, "Bourgeoisie or proletariat!" nor the ethno-Marxist claims of "White against Black"; rather, the Woke Church has readily adopted a biological Marxism of the "vaccinated versus unvaccinated."

Anti-Science and the Woke Church of the Left

While Hegel may have offered the original thesis, and Marx the antithesis, the new synthesis of the Left is biological Marxism and it's now firmly embedded into the American ethos.

> What they're talking about is the recent sprouting of an idea that's been germinating for at least 20 years in the compost heaps of feminist and Marxist political theory—the belief that science, and especially biology, is a political tool of the oppressors, mostly white male capitalists, and is therefore not to be trusted.[44]

These words, penned by journalist Peter A. Jay in an article for the *The Baltimore Sun*, warned of the dangers of the resurgence of Soviet era anti-science ideology but could have been written today. But they weren't. Jay's words written in 1997, more than a quarter of a century ago, focused on a forgotten Soviet-era biologist named Trofim Lysenko.

Lysenko, a favorite of Joseph Stalin, rejected modern biology and genetics, including the existence of DNA, in favor of a pseudo-scientific theory of heredity. Lysenko's corrupt ideas were implemented by Mao in China[45] and are at least partially to blame for the

Great Chinese Famine that claimed the lives of possibly up to 55 million people. Backed by a Marxist State, Lysenko silenced nearly all opposing scientific voices who cried foul regarding his false notions of inherited traits. Those who weren't killed by Stalin's secret police, known as the NKVD,[46] were stripped of their academic tenures and threatened.

As Jay mentioned in the article, the growth of the anti-science movement inspired by Lysenko (known as Lysenkoism) rejects modern science "as nothing more than a sexist and racist storyline created by Western white men."[47] What Jay falsely predicted, though is that "there are limits to acceptable looniness" on the Left.[48] In this new age of "scientific" understanding, there are no limits to the looniness of the Left. Boys can be girls, gender is fluid, melanin levels determine the success of an individual, and experimental vaccines are more reliable than verifiable antibodies against a virus with a recovery rate of 97 to 99.75 percent.[49]

In the absence of Stalin's secret police, today's Left must employ new enforcers of these biological Marxist ideas to silence naysayers and protect the fragile house of cards being built by neo-Lysenkoism. While it's likely that the Left will continue to use greater and greater levels of force to protect their spurious beliefs, for now, at least as far as the church is concerned, they are relying on a different weapon: morality.

CHAPTER 7

True Religion and the New Morality of the Left

A Moral Crisis

While the political Left and Right in this country rarely agree on anything, there is at least one area in which they do. Our country is in a moral crisis. If you find yourself firmly on the side of the conservative Right, the idea that progressives are concerned at all with morality might come as a shock to you, but as we will see in this chapter, they are. And maybe even more so than the Right.

Don't believe it? Just take a look at how often the Left appeals to morality when discussing policy making:

- Hilary Clinton declared families separated at the border "a moral crisis."[1]
- A Los Angeles–based Unitarian Church voted to become a sanctuary for illegal immigrants.[2]
- Rep. Alexandria Ocasio-Cortez (D-NY) also tweeted that the issue of separating families at the border is "a moral crisis."[3]

- Sen. Bernie Sanders (I-VT) stated that the government's role in the COVID-19 crisis was "an absolute moral imperative."[4]
- Rep. Nancy Pelosi (D-CA) defended America's "moral authority" at the COP26 climate summit.[5]
- Clinton, again, used the term "moral crisis," this time to describe climate change.[6]
- Rep. Ilhan Omar (D-MN) warned of an "immigration crisis" and stated that America is "losing our moral high ground" in regard to immigration.[7]

Statements like these, where the Left claims the moral high ground, may sound like political theater to conservatives, but it's important to recognize that the Left isn't being inauthentic. Contained within their words is an elite moral tapestry, constantly evolving and twisting, that they use to assume power and wage war against anyone who stands in their way. Far from the "godless party" they were once thought to be, the Woke radicals on the Left have made it abundantly clear that their sanctuary is the environment, their method of worship is sexuality, and their god is the State.

In fact, according to Emanuel Geltman, a proud socialist and a founding editor of *Dissent* magazine, one of the longest-running progressive publications in the nation, a "moral stance" is the primary thing that socialists can offer the world. (Yes, you read that right. Leading socialists believe their greatest contribution to the world is their high moral standard.)

In a 1958 article for *Dissent* arguing for nuclear disarmament, Geltman wrote:

> In a world not of their making or choice, have socialists anything to offer but a moral stance? Against the harsh realities of world politics, morality might seem to be the least effective of instruments. . . . At a moment when no other defense has yet been devised against nuclear war, political morality is

actually the last weapon left to mankind with which to save itself from destruction.[8]

In the same article, where the author wrote of "moral demand"[9] and warned that "genuine peace is impossible"[10] without "plunging the world into unimaginable horrors," we see a glimpse into the dark Gnostic infrastructure of Leftist morals. Geltman reminds us it is from this condition, that is, the total alienation of man, in which Gnostic morals are forged.

The Gnostic Morality

As we've already discussed in the first chapter, a central component to the Gnostic understanding of the universe is alienation; the state of being trapped within an oppressive system. The German existentialist Martin Heidegger, who maintained progressive views of the Christian faith throughout most of his life, called this state "thrownness."[11] That is, that man is flung into existence[12] in a world, by himself, and completely alone. The concept of thrownness can be found in virtually every ideological offshoot of Critical Theory, from Hegel's view of history and self-alienation,[13] to Charles Darwin's theory of biological competition,[14] to Marx's view of social alienation, to the Critical Race Theorist's belief in systemic racism.

For Geltman, alienation is felt in his opening lament: "In a world not of their making or choice." Like all Gnostic thinkers, Geltman viewed the world as a corrupt system that he must escape, rather than a beautiful realm to freely explore and in which to find happiness. As such, Geltman felt the elite moral framework of his socialist comrades was the only way to push back "against the harsh realities"[15] of the Western world. Even the risk of "unimaginable horrors" was no deterrent to Geltman's desire to dialectically remake the world into a new utopia. If anything, it was motivation. After all, in the mind of a socialist, the ends always justify the means.

Though written more than 60 years ago, Geltman's words could be posited today by the Left regarding any number of topics, from COVID-19 to climate change. Progressives throughout the ages, as devoted followers of the Almighty State, have accepted their mission to eradicate "unbelievers,"[16] through conversion or silence, enact laws that provide provisions for their deviant behavior, and demonstrate dominance over the people through any means necessary. While their actions are often conspicuously evil, as we will see, they perform these atrocities, not because they aren't moral or religious, but because they are.

Everything Is Sacred

"Morality has declined to a steady beat of deeper complacency. Nothing is considered pure and lovely. Nothing is sacred or enduring. Not even human life,"[17] writes a contributor for *The Press*, a publication based in the greater San Francisco Bay Area. While I agree with the author's concerns listed in the article, which is entitled "The Moral Decline of the United States of America," she is wrong in one primary way. Morals aren't in decline; they are simply changing. Now don't misunderstand, by this I don't mean that what was wrong in first-century Israel or sixteenth-century Germany is somehow mysteriously right today. This sort of nonsensical relativism goes against the very fabric of Christianity; that is, that "Jesus Christ is the same yesterday and today and forever."[18]

For the postmodern man shaped by Critical Theory and socialist ideology, it isn't that "nothing is sacred;" it's that everything is. It isn't that he doesn't have a moral code, or even that it's somehow "in decline;"[19] it's that his moral code has enlarged to such an extent that it now encapsulates virtually everything. For such a man, abortion is spiritual, same-sex love is pure, and race superiority is god-ordained. The Left's version of morality asserts, "Everything is sacred!" except for what used to be; that is, the timeless truths of the Word of God.

In this way, it's crucial that we realize that we aren't fighting against some unenlightened ignorance—the kind modern man would correct if only he were to take a course in ethics. No, the reality of the church is that we are standing before a league of grown men who previously "tasted the goodness of the Word of God and the powers of the coming age"[20] and consciously rejected it in favor of a new moral code and a religion that they invented all on their own.

Even though the book of James calls the precepts of God the "perfect law that gives freedom,"[21] the Woke Church of the Left apparently found the wide-open spaces[22] offered by the eternal Logos too restrictive and oppressive and sought to enlarge the borders and remove the gates. In this new ethical formation, the Left becomes not only the referee of morality but also the creator of the game. But lucky for us, we've seen this duel before, and it already has a name. It's called *apotheosis*.

Gods or Like God

In Christian orthodoxy, believers, through the transformative work of Christ on the cross, experience what is known as *theosis*, the Greek term for the process by which believers are "conformed into the image of his Son."[23] While there are differing opinions among denominations on when this process takes place, nearly all believe that whether in this life or the next, believers are transformed into His image and made to be like God (holy, eternal, and perfected forever).

Apotheosis, on the other hand, while not technically a direct antonym, could be described as the process of becoming, not *like* God, but *a* god. Often described more in the pantheistic theology of the New Age movement or within the doctrines of the Church of Jesus Christ of Latter-day Saints (Mormonism), apotheosis is the process by which an individual becomes a deity himself. And this is exactly what progressives ("Christian" or otherwise) are doing when they replace the principles and precepts of God with their own moral concoctions.

In strange and ludicrous irony, the Left often accuses evangelicals of believing in fairy tales. But it is progressives who have truly stopped believing in what is real. As G. K. Chesterton once wrote, "Strong and genuine religious sentiment has never had any objection to realism; on the contrary, religion was the realistic thing, the brutal thing, the thing that called names."[24]

What could be more real than declaring a boy a boy, or a girl a girl? Or recognizing that the content of a person's character is of infinitely greater importance than the color of her skin? Is it really a fairy tale to believe that all men have fallen short and are in need of a Savior? Isn't the evidence of this truth all around us? Sexual deviance, senseless riots, virus quarantine camps, and corrupt politicians fabricating lies to control the masses. Are these things not all evidence that humanity is depraved and completely incapable of redeeming itself? What is more fantastical? Calling such behavior sin, or trying to create a world where these and other activities are declared pious? Despite the obvious answer to this question, Wokeists remain determined to become gods of their own existence in an attempt to morally justify their distorted pleasures and unholy pursuits.

Absolute Truth and Moral Relativity

For the hasty critic, it would be easy to accuse Progressive Christians of moral relativism;[25] and while this may be true, it isn't the full picture. To be truly relativistic, Woke believers would be forced to respectfully acknowledge that while they don't align personally with the moral objectivity of orthodox Christianity, such beliefs may be right for those who hold them.

What we find instead is that Progressive Christians have a tendency, rather than abandoning absolute truth altogether, to redefine it. Cunningly, these new "truths" are presented as superior to the old, without question, and objectively true. That is, until the dialectic changes and a new thesis is inserted.

For example, in 2013, Pope Francis I, an outspoken advocate of Liberation Theology, addressed the "tyranny of relativism" that his predecessor, Benedict XVI, had warned against years prior. In what appeared to be a denunciation of relativism all his own, Francis explained:

> But there is another form of poverty! It is the spiritual pov-
> erty of our time, which afflicts the so-called richer countries
> particularly seriously. It is what my much-loved predecessor,
> Benedict XVI, called the "tyranny of relativism," which
> makes everyone his own criterion and endangers the coexis-
> tence of peoples. And that brings me to a second reason for
> my name. Francis of Assisi tells us we should work to build
> peace. But there is no true peace without truth! There can-
> not be true peace if everyone is his own criterion, if everyone
> can always claim exclusively his own rights, without at the
> same time caring for the good of others, of everyone, on the
> basis of the nature that unites every human being on this
> earth.[26]

In this address, Pope Francis used the language of absolute truth, condemning relativism, while simultaneously affirming the relativistic morals of Liberation Theology and globalism. Like many of the Woke Church, Francis is a master of doublespeak. He affirms the moral absolution of biblical concepts, like peace, truth, and unity, all while offering a backhanded assault against personal autonomy, equality, God-given rights, and capitalism. Though he condemns relativism, the relativism he condemns is not the same "tyranny of relativism" that Benedict XVI spoke of. The "relativism" that is egre-gious to Francis is a perceived system of inequality that allows one man to have one thing, while another goes without. In other words,

Francis isn't condemning relativism; he's condemning the alienation of the free market.

So, on one hand, Progressive Christianity has chosen the subjective over the objective, but instead of completely embracing moral relativity, in the traditional sense, the Left has constructed a new system of right and wrong where Woke ideas (like same-sex marriage and Marxism) are argued as objectively true. In other words, they reject absolute truth while claiming that their own skewed version of "truth" is . . . absolutely true.

Here are a few examples of the new moral framework of the Left at work:

- A group of abortion activists protesting in front of the Supreme Court during the *Dobbs* case publicly took abortion pills while chanting pro-choice rhetoric.[27]
- Experiments in trans-humanism expand through groups like the U.S. Defense Advanced Research Projects Agency (DARPA), who admit to working on human hybrids that can perform enhanced tasks, like "cling[ing] to the surface of a flat wall the way lizards do."[28]
- In the Netherlands, patients as young as 12 can seek assisted suicide with parental consent.[29]
- In February 2021, the U.S. House of Representatives passed the Equality Act, a bill that would likely "penalize Americans who don't affirm new sexual norms or gender ideology."[30]
- The ACLU put out a statement against fetal rights, stating that they "endanger women's rights."[31]
- Florida pastor Rodney Howard-Browne was arrested for holding church services in breach of the states' initial COVID quarantine orders in spring of 2020.[32]
- A transgender female (a male who transitioned to a "female") won a gold medal in a 2019 female weightlifting championship, eventually earning a spot in the 2020 Olympics.

- In 2017, Saudi Arabia was cheered by the world for offering citizenship to Sophia, a humanoid robot, initiating an erosion of human rights by artificial intelligence.[22]
- In a confusing back-and-forth news cycle, the Biden administration allegedly floated the idea of paying illegal immigrants separated from their families at the border up to $450,000 per family.[34]

In contrast, Biblical Christianity maintains, as a general rule, a firm belief in objective truth. That is, that there is a universal idea of what is right and what is wrong and that these notions aren't fabricated by man or culture, but they are based on the precepts and person of an eternal God. As C. S. Lewis said:

> The first thing to get clear about Christian morality between
> man and man is that in this department Christ did not
> come to preach any brand new morality. The Golden Rule
> of the New Testament is a summing up of what everyone,
> at bottom, had always known to be right. Really great moral
> teachers never do introduce new moralities: it is quacks and
> cranks who do that.[35]

Modernity may present unique and challenging ethical questions as to how to best contextualize the absolute truths of God's Word into today's culture, but a progressing culture is never justification to redefine or reposition the enduring guideposts of God's righteous standard.

Technological and medical advancements, from the safety protocols pre-programmed into driverless vehicles, AI cyborgs,[36] or curing certain illnesses through the use of controversial stem cells, will certainly force conversations about appropriating biblical truths within today's context, but they don't change these truths. Right doesn't suddenly become wrong, and wrong certainly doesn't become right. The Woke Church tries to sidestep this by claiming that its new moral standard, whether that be "Love is love" or "Equal outcomes under the law," isn't new but is simply a truer interpretation of Jesus's teachings. Against such deceitful fallacy, the church has one primary defense, and unlike the Left, it isn't morality. It's the armor of God.

The Full Armor of God

Paul's instructions in Ephesians 6 regarding the armor of God is a passage of scripture, much like the account of David slaying Goliath, that is often inadvertently reserved for lessons in children's church. For those able to momentarily suspend this judgment, they will quickly find that this passage is laced with powerful revelations regarding how to overcome deception and stand firm in the faith.

> Finally, be strong in the Lord and in His mighty power. Put on the full armor of God, so that you can take your stand against the devil's schemes. For our struggle is not against flesh and blood, but against the rulers, against the authorities, against the powers of this dark world and against the spiritual forces of evil in the heavenly realms. Therefore put on the full armor of God, so that when the day of evil comes, you may be able to stand your ground, and after you have done everything, to stand. Stand firm then, with the belt of truth buckled around your waist, with the breastplate of righteousness in place, and with your feet fitted with the readiness that comes from the Gospel of peace. In addition to all this, take up the shield of faith, with which you can extinguish all the flaming arrows of the evil one. Take the helmet of salvation and the sword of the Spirit, which is the word of God.[37]

From the beginning, Paul informs the reader that it is the "full armor of God" that makes one strong in the Lord and able to withstand the spiritual attacks and deception of the enemy. As outlined in this passage, the armor consists of:

- **Belt of Truth.** It is truth that is objective, absolute, and eternal. Or, said another way, truth is Christian orthodoxy, and it holds everything together. Without truth, there is no plumbline, or measuring stick for determining what is right or wrong. So many of the alternative Gospels and the alternative messiahs presented to the church would be easily repudiated if believers were versed in orthodoxy.

- **Breastplate of Righteousness.** This spiritual armament does two things. First, it defines the Christian's position in Christ. We are no longer simply "sinners saved by grace," but through the cross, we have been made the righteousness of God in Christ Jesus. This revelation grants us freedom from condemnation and access before God. Second, the righteousness of God reminds us that without this breastplate, we are trapped in a fallen state and spiritually depraved.

- **The Readiness of the Gospel of Peace.** The Gospel of Peace prevents the church from falling into false doctrines, such as universalism. It reminds us that there is a dying world in need of a Savior and that we are called to be not just social justice warriors but ministers of reconciliation, declaring that through the cross, God is no longer counting men's sins against them.

- **Shield of Faith.** The Shield of Faith reminds us that there is a very real battle taking place in the spiritual realm. It allows us to defend ourselves against the attacks of the devil, not simply through logic or moral actions, but through God's power made perfect in our weakness.

- **Helmet of Salvation.** More than just granting us eternal redemption, our salvation reminds us that we are a people set apart. We are in the world, but not *of* the world. Spiritual salvation protects our minds and prevents us from chasing an impossible idea of an earthly utopia by drawing our attention back to a heavenly city that will endure.
- **Sword of the Spirit.** Paul equates the Sword of the Spirit with the Word of God. This is why it's imperative that believers not participate in any system of teaching that downgrades the scriptures or discounts the miracles of the Bible, because in doing so we are rejecting God's Spirit. Without this weapon, we are powerless against the attacks of the evil one.

As globalists come closer than ever to establishing a one-world government, and war, famine, and earthquakes[38] seem to be the norm, every sign points to the reality that the Day of the Lord is drawing near. No longer can "putting on" the armor of God be viewed as optional. In his second letter to the church in Thessalonica, Paul makes it quite clear that the only way to escape the "powerful delusion" of the coming antichrist is to become a lover of the truth (emphasis added):

The coming of the lawless one will be in accordance with how Satan works. He will use all sorts of displays of power through signs and wonders that serve the lie, and all the ways that wickedness deceives those who are perishing. *They perish because they refused to love the truth and so be saved.* For this reason God sends them a powerful delusion so that they will believe the lie and so that *all will be condemned who have not believed the truth but have delighted in wickedness. . . . So* then, brothers and sisters, *stand firm and hold fast to the teachings we passed on to you, whether by word of mouth or by letter.*[39]

The truth of God's Word is our greatest protector during times of deception. As Jesus taught, "If you hold to my teaching, you are really my disciples. Then you will know the truth, and the truth will set you free."[40] Truth ultimately frees the believer from sin, sickness, shame, fear, and most importantly, eternal separation from God. In other words, truth saves us from ultimate alienation.

Alienation and the Christian

According to Christianity, the believer is not alienated from the world. He is known by God and set apart, or what scripture calls "a people holy to the Lord your God."[41] Prior to knowing Christ, the alienation that humankind experiences is not caused by the world but is as a result of sin. Describing unbelievers estranged and alienated from God, Paul writes: "They are darkened in their understanding and separated from the life of God because of the ignorance that is in them due to the hardening of their hearts."[42]

Undoubtedly a frightening place for any of us to be, Paul once again addresses the issue of alienation in the book of Colossians, but this time he offers the hope of reconciliation to God through Christ:

Once you were alienated from God and were enemies in your minds because of your evil behavior. But now he has reconciled you by Christ's physical body through death to present you holy in his sight, without blemish and free from accusation—if you continue in your faith, established and firm, and do not move from the hope held out in the Gospel. This is the Gospel that you heard and that has been proclaimed to every creature under heaven, and of which I, Paul, have become a servant.[43]

According to Paul, man's path out of alienation is not through a higher moral stance, as Geltman presented, but only by being reconciled through Christ's physical body by faith. However, this reconciliation isn't without stipulation. Note that Paul stated, "[I]f you continue in your faith," which he describes as "established and firm;" that is, if our faith remains unchanging, and that we be "not move[d] from the hope held out in the Gospel." And what is the Gospel? Paul reminds us that it is the very same Gospel that has been presented to all of creation, namely:

> For God so loved the world that He gave His one and only Son, that whoever believes in Him shall not perish but have eternal life. For God did not send his Son into the world to condemn the world, but to save the world through Him. Whoever believes in Him is not condemned, but whoever does not believe stands condemned already because they have not believed in the name of God's one and only Son. This is the verdict: Light has come into the world, but people loved darkness instead of light because their deeds were evil. Everyone who does evil hates the light, and will not come into the light for fear that their deeds will be exposed. But whoever lives by the truth comes into the light, so that it may be seen plainly that what they have done has been done in the sight of God.[44]

To understand that God gave His "one and only Son" to redeem us and free us from condemnation is only part of the equation. We also must believe that we needed saving in the first place. The first step to experiencing freedom from alienation is a recognition of our own depravity. This is where Critical Theorists and Progressives struggle, as they tend to reject the idea of original sin and blame "the system" instead of claiming personal responsibility for their own alienation from God.

Writing against an early form of Gnostic thought, John the Evangelist addresses this very thing:

> If we claim to be without sin, we deceive ourselves and the truth is not in us. If we confess our sins, He is faithful and just and will forgive us our sins and purify us from all unrighteousness. If we claim we have not sinned, we make Him out to be a liar and his word is not in us.[45]

While Progressives, Socialists, and Wokeists claim the moral high ground, Christians ironically point to their own sinfulness apart from Christ as verification of their orthodox viewpoint on morality. G. K. Chesterton described this when he so elegantly penned, "When the world goes wrong, it proves rather that the church is right. The church is justified, not because her children do not sin, but because they do."[46] Said another way, the thrownness of the world, and man's separation from God, are evidence that the Gospel of Christ is true, because it is the only message that truly rescues humanity from alienation. All other attempts at morality or redemption are futile, and all other Gospels are worthless.

Establishing a Motive

As I wrote in my last book, *The Christian Left: How Liberal Thought Has Hijacked the Church*, all sin is an attempt "to try to solve a problem either apart from God or in a way God didn't intend."[47] For the progressive, the main problem he is trying to solve is alienation. It's thrownness. Therefore, progressives strive to create a refuge for themselves, apart from God, a neo–Tower of Babel if you will, where they can assemble the last bastion of civilization to fight against an all-encompassing alienation.

Of course, this never works, which is why socialists always claim that *true* socialism has never been fully implemented. "If it had," they reason, "then it would have worked." This logic allows the

Socialist to shrug off every failed Socialist State as a far cry from "pure socialism."

But one must ask, "So what if humanity saves the environment, or the working class, if we cannot save our souls?" "So what if man is 'liberated' to express same-sex love and all of his sexual passions, if he never experiences the love of his Creator?" "Isn't separation from God, for all eternity, the greatest alienation possible?" "Shouldn't this be the primary motivation for every living and breathing human alive?"

Sadly, this is not the case, mainly due to the Left's faulty understanding and application of justice. Whether we are talking about draconian public health measures, bills to redistribute wealth, stricter EPA regulations, or diversity and equity programs, every action of the Woke is designed to maintain power and control the scales of justice. In their minds, after all, if God exists, He cannot be trusted. Suffering in the world, from illness to wage inequality, is evidence of this. Therefore, social justice, which usually amounts to nothing more than mob rule, is needed to constantly tip the scales in favor of those in perceived lack of power. At its base level, this position regarding suffering is a lack of faith in God's sovereignty. Woke Christians simply do not trust that God will indeed "rebuild the ancient ruins and restore the places long devastated,"[48] nor that faith in Him will cause those who believe to "inherit a double portion . . . and everlasting joy."[49]

Born out of this rebellious spirit, even the question, "If God is good, then why do bad things happen?" (which I addressed at length in my book *Good God: The One We Want to Believe in but Are Afraid to Embrace*)[50] is flawed from the outset and Gnostic in nature. The belief is Gnostic because within the fabric of the question is the assumption that the pain of this life is somehow attributed, whether directly or indirectly, to God. Furthermore, this sentiment is flawed, because it perceives that the choice is binary, namely, that God is either somehow good, or He isn't, and consequently lacks the Godness to do something about it.

The Left's consideration of this question, which is known as "the problem of evil,"[51] leaves them with no other choice than to take the pursuit of justice into their own hands. To expose this fully and demonstrate the superiority of God's system of justice, we'll need to venture into one of the oldest accounts of human suffering ever recorded—the book of Job.

The Book of Job

Written before the birth of Moses, the book of Job details the life of a "blameless and upright"[52] man named Job, who undergoes extreme suffering, losing virtually everything he has. The book explores themes such as God's sovereignty, patience in the face of tribulations, the authority of the devil, and divine redemption.

As I expressed in *Good God*, the book of Job is among the most misunderstood books of the Bible. Often people miss that the majority of the account is a conversation between Job and his three friends, all of whom were rebuked at the end of the book directly by God for not speaking what was true.

Perhaps the most piercing and summary words of the entire book are when God inquires of Job: "Would you discredit my justice? Would you condemn me to justify yourself?"[53] Dr. Jim Richards, an author and theologian, writes regarding God's words to Job that "every time we accept any philosophy or system of justice differing from God's justice, we are declaring, 'I am more just and fair than You!'"[54] Rather than humbling himself, Job invented doctrines in order to justify himself, even if it meant condemning God in the process.

Similar to the theology of Woke Christians, Job and his friends put forth wrong conclusions, self-righteous claims, and self-justifying accusations against God, such as:

- That Job's suffering was as a result of his sin. (Job 4:8)
- God will bless you today and curse you tomorrow. (Job 1:21)

- That the innocent never perish. (Job 4:7)
- That Job's children had sinned against God and brought judgment on themselves. (Job 8:4)
- That Job was entitled to God's deliverance because of his own innocence. (Job 10:7)
- That there is no such thing as justice. (Job 19:7)
- Job believed he had lost fellowship with God due to his negative circumstances. (Job 29:4)
- Job refused to accept that he had any wrongdoing in his own life. (Job 31)

Behind all these claims, as well as the claims of the Christian Left, is a haunting question: "Can God truly be trusted to enact and oversee justice, or must we take matters into our own hands?" Nearly all the efforts of social justice warriors, socialists, diversity and equity officers, and Woke preachers are born out of an answer to this question. They, like Job and his friends, have concluded that God cannot be trusted to carry out justice. They've decided that if justice is to be found, they must carry it out themselves. In the end, Job realized his self-righteous error, crying out:

> I know that you can do all things; no purpose of yours can be thwarted. You asked, "Who is this that obscures my plans without knowledge?" Surely I spoke of things I did not understand, things too wonderful for me to know. You said, "Listen now, and I will speak; I will question you, and you shall answer me." My ears had heard of you but now my eyes have seen you. Therefore I despise myself and repent in dust and ashes.[55]

While Job may have repented of his judgment against God, it's yet to be seen whether today's Woke Christians will be willing to do the same. Standing in the way of their repentance is often an incomplete theology of justice, one that fails to see Christianity as the most capable system for righting wrongs. But as we will see, the Bible decidedly demonstrates the unfailing justice of God, and history testifies that no other religion or philosophy can compare to the freedom, equality, and enlightenment that Christianity has introduced to the world.

CHAPTER 8

A Theology of Justice

A Spiritual Vacuum

The reticence of the modern church to tackle social issues has created a moral and spiritual vacuum in our culture, unintentionally making room for the expansion of religious pluralism. A leading justification for this silence, especially among nonconfrontational Conservative clergy, is a desire "to make the Gospel the main thing."

Author, theologian, and senior pastor of Toronto's Westminster Chapel Joseph Boot calls this "a minimalist soteriology"[1] in which evangelicals have maintained a reductionist view of the Gospel, teaching almost exclusively personal salvation, virtually without any discussion of more complex theological issues or areas of discipleship. Essentially, they speak the name of Jesus but stray away from addressing how His death, burial, and resurrection practically addresses the carnage of suffering, sin, sickness, and shame.

As a result, sensitive cultural questions are rarely sufficiently answered in light of Jesus's atonement, such as:

- Is America a racist nation?
- Are homosexuality and Christianity compatible?
- Does the Bible support climate change?
- Are race reparations biblical?
- Was Jesus a socialist?
- Does loving your neighbor mean being in favor of open borders?
- Would Jesus support universal health care?
- Do I need to repent of my ancestors' transgressions?

The church leaders who have spoken boldly on the social issues listed above have not done so without repercussions. These individuals have faced a tremendous onslaught of judgmental labels from Woke Christians and secular media calling them out of touch,[2] sectarian,[3] bigoted,[4] and intolerant.[5]

In most cases, the accusations toward these brave souls are unfounded, but it's important to recognize the growing concern among progressives that the church lost her compassion as she tightened her grip on orthodoxy. In other words, she may be right, but sometimes she's mean.

So while the brave few are willing to address such topics, unless they do so from a position that accounts for the cross, such discussions will never elicit systemic and lasting change. Even though Conservative Christian pastors and leaders may understand what is wrong, their lack of empathy and connection to the complete salvific work of the cross creates a failure to understand practically how we get right.

One of the more public examples of this took place in Mount Juliet, Tennessee, where Pastor Greg Locke warned his congregation, "If . . . you start showing up (with) all these masks and all this nonsense . . . I will ask you to leave. I am not playing these Democrat games up in this church."[6] While many conservatives may agree with Locke's sentiments, his delivery was unquestionably off.[7]

Another Tennessee pastor went viral after preaching a message entitled, "Why Leviticus 20:13 Should Still Be Enforced," in reference to reinstating the death penalty for homosexuals. When interviewed the next week about his extreme position, this pastor told reporters: "I am over this. I am the head of this church. I say who comes and goes. Those people are not permitted to join, those people are not permitted to attend."[8] Locke's statements about masks may have been poorly crafted, but this pastor's ranting was toxic. Is homosexuality a sin? Of course. But it does the kingdom no good to maintain an orthodox position about a particular social issue if we lose our grasp on the purpose of the cross in the process. Such obvious folly needs to be avoided.

Examples such as these have created a window of opportunity for Progressive Christianity, which shouts a resounding "yes" to all of the cultural questions listed above, with no concern for what scripture these affirmations violate. As Boot describes, "They offer 'social justice,' in the name of the reign and mission of God—a new friendly Christianity that welcomes doctrinal change, embraces diversity and seeks to right the wrongs in the structures of society."[9] In the same way that some staunch evangelical Christians only care about the truth, with little concern for mercy or grace, Progressive Christians have demonstrated a strong willingness to abandon the truth altogether if it helps the fight against inequity and injustice.

Woke Theology Is Built Upon a System of Injustice

The writer of Proverbs reminds us, "Differing weights and differing measures—the Lord detests them both."[10] In the marketplace in ancient Israel, primitive scales were used to measure the amount of items purchased, whether they be spices, grains, or precious metals. Unsavory shop owners intentionally used inaccurate weights in order to cheat the customer and tip the scales in their favor. Currently, Wokeists are far from possessing a definition of justice that is free from partiality and judgments based on gender, race, and socioeconomic markers. Critical Race Theory, identity politics, and COVID-19 policies are all guilty of utilizing differing scales of partiality and justice. Here are just a few examples of differing weights and measures celebrated by Wokeism today:

- Different requirements for patrons based on vaccination status.
- Lowering the demands of academic performance for students based on race or skin color.
- Failure to prosecute rioters, looters, or illegal migrants based on race.
- The mainstream media possess two different standards of behavior and vocabulary, depending upon political party (e.g., When Trump said "China virus," it was xenophobic, but when Dr. Fauci used the term "Wuhan strain," it was acceptable.)[11]
- Leftist elites, such as Joe Biden, Nancy Pelosi, and Gavin Newsom, parade around in public and at private parties without masks, all while requiring others to wear them.
- Progressives claim to champion women's rights, yet applaud transgender women (biological males) for competing in female sports.

The Woke Left interminably show themselves to be the party of "rules for thee, but not for me," as they create two sets of policies, one for the people and one for them. At the time this book went to press, behaviors like these drove rumors of a political "red wave" rising across America ahead of the 2022 mid-term election cycle, as conservative candidates hoped to overturn existing Democratic seats throughout the nation, especially in key swing states. But more than creating political fallout, the double-standard morality of the Left reveals their greatest secret: the party of diversity, equity, and inclusion actually promotes injustice regardless of the outcome of elections.

According to Woke ideology, a just society is one where there is an equal distribution of goods, and the war against systematic oppression is perpetually waged.[12] The Heritage Foundation divulges that the equal distribution of goods goes beyond just "bare necessities" and could include everything from equal "income; employment opportunities; wealth; property ownership; housing; education . . ." to even "more intangible goods" like "political power," "political participation," and "social recognition."[13] In fact, the war against systematic oppression is expanded to include the dismantling of any system that allows those in power to "consistently benefit directly or indirectly from the others' disadvantages."[14]

Reading through a list like this, one can understand the appeal of Marxism. But similar to the English mathematician and physicist Isaac Newton's third law of motion, every action will always produce an equal and opposite reaction. What Woke idealists fail to explain is that the redistribution of wealth, opportunity, or power will always lead to an "opposite reaction" of stealing wealth, opportunity, or power from those who have earned it through hard work and the free market. Ryan Messmore addresses this and other downsides of the social justice movement, in what he called the "counterproductive" focus of "mitigating" inequality:

> They are born of a misconception rooted in a flawed understanding of both justice and economic fact. Even if their premises and objectives were sound, these policies would have perverse unintended consequences—fostering class resentment, destroying jobs and reducing wages and opportunities for the poor most of all. Such policies also tend to undermine the family and create a culture of dependence on the state—unleashing harmful consequences that would, again, fall disproportionately on the poor.[15]

In other words, while the Left thinks they are fighting injustices, they are actually creating them. The Marxist elite likely understand this and are using the perceived increasing gaps in society between Blacks and Whites, rich and poor, young and old, to drive a wedge in the support walls of Western democracy. Dr. Jim Richards issues a strong indictment against the complicity of Leftist elites who knowingly create such divisive conditions within society:

> Are we so naive as to think the leaders in Cuba, China, Venezuela and other countries were unaware that their policies would thrust their citizens into financial desperation and poverty? Of course, they knew! It was part of their strategy to bring about a shift in wealth and power from the citizens to the elitists! Leaders making a grab for power and money always know the destruction their policies will bring. Yet, they have total disregard for those who will be negatively affected! This is the mindset of an elitist![16]

The social justice warriors, on the other hand (that is, the boots on the ground fighting perceived injustice, both in and out of the church), are likely clueless about the greater detriments and societal repercussions that their work is generating. If they recognized the downsides, they'd undoubtedly stop their efforts, as I truly believe the majority are moved by sincerity to "make a difference."

This is one reason, I believe, that conservative advocacy groups established on Judeo-Christian principles, like PragerU, the Heritage Foundation, and Family Research Council, are having so much success converting well-intended liberals, especially those belonging to the Millennial and Gen Z generations, into conservatives. PragerU alone boasts that its educational content has received over five billion lifetime views and has changed millions of lives.

This is a huge win for conservatism, but there is still tremendous work left to do. If we are to win such individuals back to the truth, then the church must strive to rediscover and present a definition of justice that is vastly superior to the fabricated sense of security and empty utopian promises generated by Woke leaders. Such a solution cannot be only political or merely moral, and must address all injustices across space and time. Requirements like these leave us only one place to look: the death, burial, and resurrection of Jesus Christ.

A Practical Solution for Evil

As Wokeism comes up short on delivering any form of societal justice, a need arises within the church to recover a renewed vision of justice, one that offers redemption from the Fall and reconciles the pain and suffering of the world. The temptation in the church is to look for this solution within American conservatism rather than in Christ Himself.

The tenets of capitalism, American exceptionalism, and libertarian ideologies offer much from a humanistic perspective that could alleviate the temporary ills of society, even those created by socialism. But, ultimately, these too will fall dramatically shy of offering any permanent solution to the problem of evil. The reason for this is that the remedy for evil is not found within the ranks of humanity, because fundamentally humanity is the habitation of the problem. Theologian N. T. Wright explains:

> Evil, I argued, isn't just a philosophical problem but a practical one ... that Western democracy itself isn't to be thought of as an automatic solution to the problem of global evil, and that we need to take seriously both the supra-human powers of evil and the fact that the line between good and evil runs not between "us" and "them" but through every individual and every society.[17]

As Wright conveys, philosophical theories, such as those offered by Hegel or Marx, or even Republicanism for that matter, fail to address the spiritual origin of evil and, therefore, no matter how good a philosophy they may be, these theories serve only as a Band-Aid at best. One theory might address the issues slightly better than the other, but neither will stop the bleeding if the artery is ruptured. This arterial line, which Wright described as a line running "through every individual and every society," is the line of sin. Until sin is addressed spiritually, there can be no complete eradication of evil and certainly no true justice.

Conservatives, of whom I am one, wrongly conclude at times that if only abortion can be ended, Critical Race Theory removed from schools, and every socialist tarred and feathered, then the American way would be free once again to heal the world. As a patriot and a conservative, I would like nothing more than for each of these to come to pass and feel that through these actions the world *would* be a better place. But even if conservatism gains ground, sin will remain, and justice will be found wanting.

Wright calls this "the myth of progress;"[18] that is, that if we can only keep progressing more closely to "our" preferred world, then utopia will be found. This is the error of Critical Theory we've been discussing all along, but it's also the error of godless conservatism. Wright reminds us, "Imagining a world without evil is not simply imagining what things would be like if we could only work a bit harder and arrive at the utopia that we all know is just around the corner."

The Christian solution, and really the only solution that practically addresses the existence of evil and the redemptive needs of a creation that is subjected to sin and death, is the death and resurrection of Christ. What else can right wrongs, remove shame, undo the curse of death, bind the devil, and bridge the chasm caused by sin? Wright recalled for us that "Jesus Christ and him crucified"[19] is our only option:

> According to the early Christians, what was accomplished
> in Jesus's death and resurrection is the foundation, the
> model and the guarantee for God's ultimate purpose, which
> is to rid the world of evil altogether and to establish his new
> creation of justice, beauty and peace.[20]

The guarantee, as Wright referred to it, provided by the death and resurrection of Jesus, means that the cross isn't just the answer for our personal salvation, but for our total salvation—spirit, soul, and body. Same-sex attraction, marital problems, racism, disease, and anger issues are all practically addressed "by grace through faith"[21] by the cross of Christ. In fact, any attempt to solve these issues, without first filtering the solution through the cross, is contradictory to the plans and purposes of God. The Apostle Paul elucidated this point in Romans 12:17-21 (NIV):

> Do not repay anyone evil for evil. . . . Do not take revenge, my dear friends, but leave room for God's wrath, for it is written: "It is mine to avenge; I will repay," says the Lord. On the contrary: "If your enemy is hungry, feed him; if he is thirsty, give him something to drink. In doing this, you will heap burning coals on his head." Do not be overcome by evil, but overcome evil with good.

According to Romans, God alone possesses absolute jurisdiction over justice, including the carrying out of wrath against evil. The methodology of the Woke robs God of this jurisdiction and places the scales of justice and the power for vengeance into the hands of men, to carry out judgments against evil, both real and fabricated.

As Christians, our part is to "overcome evil with good," and we do this by practically demonstrating the reconciliatory aspects of the cross into every dark corner of society. This grants us a working theology capable of offering to everyone, regardless of their place in life, a pervasive and complete framework for justice. A framework that reveals every person is simultaneously both the oppressed *and* the oppressor; it removes all "us vs. them" language from our vocabulary and exposes that "Jews and Gentiles alike are all under the power of sin."[22] As we will see, it is this understanding, that "all [men] have sinned and fallen short of the glory of God," that sits as a foundational starting block for developing a biblical theology of justice.

God: Our Theology of Justice

"He is the Rock, his works are perfect, and all his ways are just. A faithful God who does no wrong, upright and just is he,"[23] wrote Moses, inspired by the Spirit of God. Throughout the pages of the Bible, verses like these accumulate to form a systematic theology of justice based on the self-revelation of the Creator-God.

A theology of justice could be summarized as:

1. Humans are depraved, and their justice is flawed.
2. Only God is just.
3. Apart from God, no justice exists.
4. Due to man's free will, injustice is temporarily allowed to exist on the earth.
5. The death, burial, and resurrection of Jesus Christ enacted God's plan for complete and total justice, both now and forever.
6. On the last day, God will issue righteous judgment against all iniquity, resulting in perfect justice.
7. Those found in Christ shall enter into a realm of eternal bliss.
8. Evildoers, fallen angels, and the devil himself shall be cast out into a realm of eternal punishment.

To abbreviate this sequence even further, a theology of justice could be condensed by merely pulling from James's epistle: "There is only one Lawgiver and Judge, the one who is able to save and destroy. But you—who are you to judge your neighbor?"[24] Or perhaps by taking comfort in Isaiah's words, "For the Lord is our judge, the Lord is our lawgiver, the Lord is our king; it is he who will save us."[25]

This framework for justice, which depends on God as our source, is often passed over by the Left in lieu of their own brand of justice. Consider the case of Lia Thomas, a biological male, who is competing as a transgendered woman in collegiate swimming. As a male, Lia was All–Ivy League during a previous season and is now, after transitioning to "female," crushing "her" new competition. To the Woke's Left, this is a victorious moment in women's athletics, but Lia's teammates are rightly outraged and discouraged over the unfairness of a biological male competing as a female. One of Lia's team members shared anonymously, as reported by Faithwire.com, that her other teammates "feel so discouraged because no matter how much work they put into it, they're going to lose."[26] As Woke universities attempt to bring about their own twisted form of justice, the scriptures offer an alternative method: faith.

The writer of Hebrews also adds to this doctrinal tapestry of justice when he puts forward, "And without faith it is impossible to please God, because anyone who comes to Him must believe that He exists and that He rewards those who earnestly seek Him."[27]

Although the word "justice" doesn't appear in this passage, it's nonetheless central to the concept of faith in Christ. If God doesn't exist, then no wrongs can be made right. Likewise, if God isn't good; that is, if He doesn't reward those who seek Him, then even if He does exist, His existence will never grant justice to His children. True faith trusts God to make good on His promises, including rewarding those who believe in Him and punishing evildoers.

The Bible warns, though, that man will not always rely on God to make things right. In Luke 18, Jesus predicts a day when humankind will lose faith in God's justice. Luke recounts the story as follows:

> Then Jesus told his disciples a parable to show them that they should always pray and not give up. He said: "In a certain town there was a judge who neither feared God nor cared what people thought. And there was a widow in that town who kept coming to him with the plea, 'Grant me justice against my adversary.' For some time he refused. But finally he said to himself, 'Even though I don't fear God or care what people think, yet because this widow keeps bothering me, I will see that she gets justice, so that she won't

eventually come and attack me!'" And the Lord said, "Listen to what the unjust judge says. And will not God bring about justice for his chosen ones, who cry out to him day and night? Will he keep putting them off? I tell you, he will see that they get justice, and quickly. However, when the Son of Man comes, will he find faith on the earth?"[28]

Faith for what? Based on the parable, Jesus was wondering whether or not upon His return there would be any left who still believed that God would bring about justice for His chosen ones. In eerie similarity, this is exactly what social justice encapsulates with its belief in man's alienation: a belief that he has been left alone with no one to enact justice but himself.

Is the silent premise of the social justice movement, and every other form of Critical Theory, that we must equip the oppressed to rise up and seek recompense, reparations, and retaliation against their oppressors? Currently, cities such as Asheville,[29] Evanston,[30] and Tulsa[31] are embracing this, as they each take steps to institute reparations to some of their city's residents. Likely, this is just the beginning of what is to come.

Have we become so disconnected with truth and grace that we've forgotten that the cross of Christ is the point of intersectionality, in which judgment against sin was issued, and that now the church simply waits for the promise of eternal justice to be fulfilled?

If we are to recover the Gospel of the cross and have any chance of winning back the Woke culture, even more than a theology of justice, we will need to know the person of justice, Christ Himself, who gave His life, exchanging our depravity for His righteousness, in a perfect manifestation of grace and truth.

Justice: An Expression of Grace and Truth

The first chapter of the book of John discloses of Jesus: "The Word became flesh and made His dwelling among us. We have seen His glory, the glory of the one and only Son, who came from the Father, full of grace and truth." Because Jesus is at the epicenter of biblical justice, we must take seriously our understanding of grace and truth. Every false variant of justice errs by elevating either grace or truth over one another, thus distancing themselves from the person of Christ. Only by ensuring that both are fully present and accounted for within our framework of justice can we discern whether or not we are in error.

In John, Jesus displays a consummate combination of grace and truth in His exchange with the Pharisees and the woman caught in the act of adultery:

> The teachers of the law and the Pharisees brought in a woman caught in adultery. They made her stand before the group and said to Jesus, "Teacher, this woman was caught in the act of adultery. In the Law Moses commanded us to stone such women. Now what do you say?" They were using this question as a trap, in order to have a basis for accusing him. But Jesus bent down and started to write on the ground with his finger. When they kept on questioning him, he straightened up and said to them, "Let any one of you who is without sin be the first to throw a stone at her." Again he stooped down and wrote on the ground. At this, those who heard began to go away one at a time, the older ones first, until only Jesus was left, with the woman still standing there. Jesus straightened up and asked her, "Woman, where are they? Has no one condemned you?" "No one, sir," she said. "Then neither do I condemn you," Jesus declared. "Go now and leave your life of sin."[32]

In sheer spiritual brilliance, Jesus refused to excuse the woman's ungodly behavior but instead silenced her accusers by exposing their own depravity. This allowed Him the time to then minister to her in grace, empowering her to rise above her situation and leave her life of sin. Rarely do we witness such ingenious displays of grace and truth working hand-in-hand. More commonly, we find polarized extremes of either minimizing unrighteousness or locking arms with the Pharisees to throw the first stone. Neither meets the qualifications for true justice that Jesus embodies.

Jesus, again, takes us to this same intersection of grace and truth in both His conversation with Zaccheus and His encounter with the Samaritan woman at the well in John 4. In the case of Zaccheus, He didn't even have to issue a rebuke. His sheer presence was enough to bring justice to the chief tax collector's victims, as Zaccheus cried out in repentance, "Look, Lord! Here and now I give half of my possessions to the poor, and if I have cheated anybody out of anything, I will pay back four times the amount."[33] In all three accounts, it was the person of Jesus, the Word made flesh (not His actions nor moral standing), that alone emanated justice.

This is why the elements of communion, or the Eucharist as it is known, are indispensable for the Christian. More than a compulsory religious act, communion serves as a constant reminder of God's justice through Christ. The elements themselves, the bread and the wine, point us not just to His acts but to His body and blood, reminding us that through the cross we do not receive the punishment that our sins deserve but instead have been granted eternal life through faith in His name. In this, we see the grace and truth of Christ. Grace displayed through the forgiveness of our sins that His death granted us, and truth that compels us to acknowledge that we are sinners who need Christ's salvation in order to even receive the elements.

Seeing the sacrificial person of Jesus in the elements of communion, that is, His body and blood, instead of sanctimony, has proven hard for Woke Christians. Demonstrating a total failure to understand the role of the sacraments, progressive priest Fr. Jerome R. Secillano addressed the topic of the Eucharist in a piece entitled "Why the Eucharist Promotes Social Justice," stating, "The Eucharist is essentially about the acknowledgment of oppression" where "all are given the opportunity to lament, to understand the hurts we have caused and to come face-to-face with the need to be just and morally upright."[34] Secillano, who goes on to mention the collective and inclusive aspects of the sacraments, like most Wokeists, misses the point completely and makes the cross about his own morality rather than the power of God.

In case a reminder is needed, Jesus said, "This is my body, which is for you; do this in remembrance of me."[35] As humankind, we aren't the progenitors of justice. Any good works that we display or carry out must find their source and power in Christ alone. As we approach the sacraments, we remember Christ, not ourselves. We see His actions, not ours. Social justice imitates and replicates the works of Jesus, His actions, but disdains the divinity behind the deeds.

The Apostle Paul cautioned believers of individuals such as these, who would arise in the last days, boasting of their good works, but deny the power of God, writing (emphasis added):

> But mark this: *There will be terrible times in the last days.* People will be lovers of themselves, lovers of money, boastful, proud, abusive, disobedient to their parents, ungrateful, unholy, without love, unforgiving, slanderous, without self-control, brutal, not lovers of the good, treacherous, rash, conceited, lovers of pleasure rather than lovers of God— *having a form of godliness but denying its power.* Have nothing to do with such people. They are the kind who worm their way into homes and gain control over gullible women, who are loaded down with sins and are swayed by all kinds of evil desires, *always learning but never able to come to a knowledge of the truth.* Just as Jannes and Jambres opposed Moses, so also these teachers oppose the truth. *They are men of depraved minds, who, as far as the faith is concerned, are rejected.* But they will not get very far because, as in the case of those men, their folly will be clear to everyone.[36]

Paul's indictment against these "men of depraved minds," known by "having a form of godliness but denying its power," could not be a better descriptor of the Woke Christian Left. While they talk of justice, service, caring for the poor and the immigrant, they reject the source of God's power, namely, the grace and truth of the person of Jesus who is the living and breathing testament of the Gospel. As Paul writes, "For the message of the cross is foolishness to those who are perishing, but to us who are being saved it is the power of God."[37]

St. Augustine called this "the standard of falsehood," in which men reject the plan and purposes of God, in order to create their own definitions of righteousness and justice. Augustine reminds us that injustice is not the fault of God, who created men "right," but the blame falls solely upon humanity who abandoned God's plan, for their own "Gospel." For individuals, such as transgender athlete Lia Thomas or even those pushing for reparations in cities like Asheville, Evanston, and Tulsa, Augustine has this to offer:

> The fact is that man was created right, on condition that he should live by the standard of his creator, not by his own, carrying out not his own will, but his creator's. Falsehood consists in not living in the way for which he was created.[38]

After man abandoned the truth for falsehood, God's justice left Him no other option than to punish sin in sinful man. But while God's justice required that a sacrifice be made to atone for the sins of a fallen people, His love demanded that He Himself take our place. Truth and grace, beautifully and perfectly manifested in the body and blood of the Lord Jesus Christ. He gave Himself up on our behalf, to face death on a cross, so that we might live.

The cross, therefore, is the great equalizer. All men, saints and sinners, oppressors and oppressed, Blacks and Whites, young and old, slave and free, find themselves on the same footing and, apart from Christ, all equally deserving of death.

Keep in mind, the cross wasn't an afterthought. It was always plan A. The Bible teaches that from the beginning of time, God had in mind to send Christ as the propitiation for our sins. In Revelation 13:8, John discloses, "the Lamb who was slain from the creation of the world." From the very beginning, God was overseeing His creation to ensure that justice would be accomplished through the second person of the Trinity, Jesus Christ. That's why it is essential that we set out on a new quest for the Biblical Christ.

CHAPTER 9

The Quest for
the Biblical Christ

A New Quest Is Needed

From Critical Theory to Liberation Theology, a common motif that underpins these philosophies is a mostly terrestrial view of Jesus. With few exceptions, Jesus of Nazareth is little more than a countercultural social worker with an altruistic outlook on life who challenged the social norms and traditional thinkers of His time. Within these ideologies, the power of Jesus is limited. Far from the Eternal Word made flesh, performing signs and wonders through the power of God, He is a limp Messiah whose works and words are watered down, secularized, and the effects of which are limited to the first century. Biblical stories like the Sermon on the Mount or Jesus flipping over the tables of the moneychangers provide progressive theologians with the historical materials necessary to craft a convincing social Gospel with meager biblical support.

As we've already discussed, these theories of a secular Christ are not as sound as the Left would like to think. Like most evangelicals,

Craig S. Keener, author of *The Historical Jesus of the Gospels*, came to the conclusion that "the basic portrayal of Jesus in the first-century Gospels . . . is more plausible than the alternative hypotheses of its modern detractors."[1]

This means that while Albert Schweitzer and his modern Christian Left counterparts, whether they be Black Lives Matter activists or Woke Southern Baptists, may have embarked on their quest for the Historical Jesus nobly. They ultimately arrived at the wrong destination and fell markedly short of ever identifying the true Christ. In light of these innumerable failed attempts to compose a bona fide portrait of the true Historical Jesus, it seems only right to reclaim the spirit of the quest by searching in places unthinkable to the former questers: the Holy Scriptures and Christian orthodoxy. Let our quest for the Biblical Christ begin.

In past quests, it seems some biographers sought Jesus's identity everywhere but the scriptures and the early apostolic Christian tradition themselves. More specifically, when they did consider the scriptures, they rarely examined passages outside of the Synoptic Gospels (Matthew, Mark, and Luke) and the fictitious Gospel of Q, avoiding almost entirely the books of John, Acts, and Revelation and key epistles by Paul, which all offer concrete evidence of Jesus's existence and divinity. Also, conveniently absent from the work of Historical Jesus biographers are any significant investigations of Old Testament passages and prophecies that point to Jesus as the pre-existent Word of God found in Genesis, Exodus, Isaiah, and Daniel.

To properly understand why the former quests lacked research from the exhaustive amounts of biblical sources and verified documents from the second-, third-, and fourth-century Christian writers—some of whom, like Clement, Ignatius, and Irenaeus of Lyons, have direct connection to Jesus's disciples—that offer invaluable insights into the earliest accounts of Jesus and the nature of the Gospel would require an entire book of its own.

With that said, due to the weakness of the arguments found collectively within Progressive and Critical Theology that point to a human Jesus rather than a glorified Lord, my hope is that this chapter will prove sufficient to repudiate the counterfeit "Woke Jesus" and provide ample evidence of the true Messiah, the God-Man Jesus Christ, who is the King of kings and Lord of lords. To begin this quest, we must start in the beginning in the book of Genesis.

In the Beginning

Within the scriptures of Genesis 1 are divine artifacts, testifying from the beginning of time to the presence, alongside the Father and the Spirit, of the pre-existent Christ, the Word of God. While the earth was still "formless and empty"[2] Genesis says, God spoke. The catalyst for all of creation, the Word went forth, eternally begotten, from the mouth of the Father, pushing back darkness and filling the void. Shattering all fallacies that Jesus was only human, Paul apostolically asserts that it was Jesus who was present with God from the beginning of time:

> The Son is the image of the invisible God, the firstborn over all creation. For in him all things were created: things in heaven and on earth, visible and invisible, whether thrones or powers or rulers or authorities; all things have been created through him and for him. He is before all things, and in him all things hold together.[3]

In John's Gospel, Jesus Himself confirms this same reality regarding His own pre-existence and eternal nature, boldly affirming, "Before Abraham was born, I am!"[4] In his classic work, *A Theology of the New Testament*, renowned Christian scholar George Eldon Ladd expounded upon the meaning of Jesus's words here, writing, "This amazing affirmation is an allusion to the Old Testament usage. God revealed himself to Moses as 'I am who I am.'"[5] Ladd went on to show that the Lord's "pre-existence is also predicated in Jesus's last prayer: 'Father, glorify thou me with the glory which I had with thee before the world was made.'"[6]

Early progressive theologians, like Johannes Weiss, dismissed passages like these, claiming they were "influenced by Paulinism"[7] and existed apart from the Synoptic Gospels. Ladd, setting the record straight, obliterated these claims, stating, "Jesus's very use of the term Son of Man involved an implicit claim to pre-existence. The Johannine Jesus[8] only affirms more explicitly what is implicit in the Synoptics."[9] Here are just a few examples of the implicit language Ladd had in mind within the Synoptic Gospels that points to Jesus's pre-existence:

- In Matthew 1:21-23, Jesus is referred to as "Immanuel," meaning "God with us."
- In Mark 1:1, Jesus is called "the Son of God."
- In Mark 1:21-28, an evil spirit recognizes Jesus and cries out, "I know who you are—the Holy One of God!"
- In Mark 2:5-12, Jesus forgives a man's sins and then confirms His authority to do so by healing the man.
- In Mark 2:17, Jesus uses the Greek word *érchomai* in reference to His coming into the world. The word means "to come from one place to another," implying that Jesus came from one place (heaven) to fulfill a purpose in another place (earth). This same root word is also used in Luke 7:18-23 and Luke 12:49-51.
- In Mark 12:6-8, Jesus tells a parable about a son being sent by His father to check on his vineyard, paralleling His being sent by the Father into the world to save the world.
- In Mark 4:35-41, Jesus takes authority over the wind and waves, thus demonstrating His deity.

Any one of these passages within the Synoptic Gospels is enough to validate and support the Johannine and Pauline doctrine of Jesus's pre-existence and divinity. Together, though, these verses form staggering evidence that Jesus, His disciples, and the Apostle Paul all taught and believed that the "Son of Man" not only predated Abraham, but that He was with God in the beginning.

While theologically imperative, establishing the pre-existence of Christ is also practically important to understanding God's view of sin and judgment and what that means for us as people of faith. Recognizing Jesus for who He is, the Lamb of God slain from the foundation of the world, obliges us to make sense of His life and death. If Jesus was only a man, perhaps a mystic or even an apocalyptic prophet as many Woke teachers propose, His death, albeit tragic, means little. But if Jesus is the Christ, the begotten Son of God, then His sacrifice on the cross reveals much! To understand its full significance, we turn first to investigate the incarnation itself.

Made in Human Likeness

Born of a virgin, Jesus entered this world, forsaking the glories of heaven in exchange for a life of certain pain and suffering. Paul vividly described the process and agonizing ramifications of Christ's decision to take on flesh and blood:

> Who, being in very nature God, did not consider equality
> with God something to be used to His own advantage;
> rather, He made Himself nothing by taking the very nature
> of a servant, being made in human likeness. And being
> found in appearance as a man, He humbled Himself by
> becoming obedient to death—even death on a cross![10]

As the second person of the Trinity, Jesus, as Paul says, "being in very nature God," had every right to enter this earth with glorious fanfare, but He didn't. Instead, as the Holman Christian Standard Bible puts it, "He emptied Himself by assuming the form of a slave."[11]

Far from the handsome and charismatic man He's often depicted as in the movies, Jesus entered this world as a thankless servant and not a Hollywood hunk. According to Isaiah, the incarnate Christ "had no beauty or majesty to attract us to Him, nothing in His appearance that we should desire Him."[12] In this way, Jesus gave up His glory and left behind His majesty "so that by His death He might break the power of Him who holds the power of death—that is, the devil—and free those who all their lives were held in slavery by their fear of death."[13]

Never can Jesus be accused of not understanding our plight or not knowing what it's like to walk in our shoes. If anything, from a human perspective, apart from possibly the precious martyrs throughout the years who paid the ultimate price for their faith, most of us will never know what it was like for Him to endure so much pain and abuse. According to the prophet Isaiah, even before His torment on the cross, Jesus "was despised and rejected by mankind, a man of suffering, and familiar with pain. Like one from whom people hide their faces He was despised, and we held Him in low esteem."[14] None of this was for naught, though, because the humble entrance of Jesus provided the covert covering necessary to hide His identity long enough to accomplish God's plan.

The Mystery Revealed

While the Old Testament and the prophets testify to the coming Messiah, their language was shrouded enough that it was only by faith that someone could discern God's plan and timing. Paul called this "God's secret wisdom"[15] and explained it as "a mystery that has been hidden and that God destined for our glory before time began."[16] Continuing, Paul adds just how veiled God's plan was: "None of the rulers of this age understood it, for if they had, they would not have crucified the Lord of glory."[17] It was never God's intent, though, to keep Jesus hidden forever. In fact, had the identity of Christ stayed hidden, Christianity, like Critical Theory, wouldn't be much different from Gnosticism. Thankfully, though, in what Paul describes in Colossians as "when the set time had fully come,"[18]

God made known "the mystery that has been kept hidden for ages and generations, but is now disclosed to the Lord's people . . . which is Christ in you, the hope of glory."[19]

For the Gnostic, public disclosure of mysteries of any kind goes against their grain. It's contradictory to their nature. As writer and philanthropist Roberta Green Ahmanson reminds us, "Gnosticism was always an elitist enterprise."[20] Due to this tendency, Christian Gnostics tend to see the disclosure of the mysteries of God as privy only to the elite class, not something that you could trust with the common man. They also struggled with the incarnation, because they believed that the divine and the carnal could never commingle. For this reason, most Gnostics rejected the idea of the incarnation, preferring a view that Jesus was a man with secret revelation rather than God incarnate.

Though modified for modernity, this same view persists among Progressive Christians today who minimize "the Christ" as a man and elevate the social ministry of Jesus over the spiritual work of the Kingdom. Others, like Brandon West, the creator of Project Global Awakening, twist the mystery of the incarnation and the eventual indwelling of the Holy Spirit to mean that we are all God-incarnate, thus reducing the uniqueness of Jesus Himself. West, in an article for ProgressiveChristianity.org, offered this:

> When are we going to understand that when Jesus said,
> "You are Gods," he meant, that we are all Gods. Our true
> nature is not form, it is pure energy which is consciousness.
> We are God-consciousness who has incarnated into this
> level of reality, but we have become so identified with mate-
> rial form that we forgot our original nature.[21]

The more Christ's uniqueness is trivialized, the less the Gnostic has to deal with His divinity. As long as "we are all Christ," then nothing has to be done with *the* Christ. If everything is holy and spiritual, then nothing is.

Of course, not every progressive's faith is mangled to the point where they think themselves Christ, but even subtleties in this realm can be damaging. For instance, Martin Hughes, an atheist and writer at Patheos who covers topics related to Christianity, in an article entitled "Everyone in the World is Christ, and They Are All Crucified," had this to say:

> I don't believe there's evidence for a conscious being named "God," or that Jesus really rose from the dead. But I think there might be a helpful metaphor here, maybe, that could build a bridge between my own position and that of many Christians. . . . We're innocent as the mythological Christ, but the way society sees us makes us look guilty (and feel guilty when we internalize it), and if the production of that guilt is what "crucifies" us, and if the production of that guilt could be labeled "sin," then, in that sense, if you think about it, we're all Christ, and we're all dying for the sins of the world.[22]

Confessing his intention in writing the piece, Hughes stated that his goal was to "build a bridge between [his] own position and that of many Christians." From an atheist viewpoint, this is respectable, but as Christians, this is another story.

Undoubtedly, Christians should look for areas of common ground to build a bridge to reach and minister to those whom they encounter. Paul did this at Mars Hill in Athens in Acts 17 when he referenced the Athenians' altar to the unknown god.[23] Using the culture of the people, scripture records that Paul successfully led some of his hearers to Christ, including a member of the Areopagus named Dionysius, a woman named Damaris, and several others.[24] But let's be clear: Hughes's "bridge" isn't one of these moments.

When progressives, like Hughes, speak of bridges, it's important to note, they usually only allow one-way traffic. His argument might be constructed using Christian terminology, but his conclusions are anything but. Man isn't innocent, Christ isn't a myth, spiritual guilt isn't a social construct: a sinful man can never bear the weight of the sin of the whole world. Hughes isn't asking for joint understanding; he's calling for believers to compromise their faith. For Christians to make any agreement with Hughes on these topics would be to deny not only the incarnation of Christ but the cross as well.

To protect ourselves against this progressive and metaphorical view of Christ, as well as other similar tactics of the Left, we must push forward in our quest to recognize the importance of not only Christ's incarnation but His death as well.

Christus Victor

In his fight for orthodoxy within the early church, the patristic father Irenaeus of Lyons needed a way to refute the Gnostic teachings about Jesus that were infiltrating and confusing the second-century ecclesia. In the time of Irenaeus, the Gnostic's view of Christ varied between those who held that He was a spiritual being who only appeared human and those who believed Him to be a man after the flesh who somehow obtained a secret knowledge of God. Either view, according to Irenaeus, was heretical. To combat this, the Bishop of Lyons needed a way to demonstrate how the Spirit (divinity) and flesh (humanity) of Christ were both necessary (in cooperation with one another) in order to completely defeat the power of the devil and redeem humankind from sin and death. Irenaeus found the explanation he needed in what became known as the "theory of recapitulation."

The theory of recapitulation, also known as the "classic view of Atonement" and/or "Christus Victor,"[25] is one of several theories of atonement that are used by theologians to explain the process by which God redeems mankind through Christ. First formally posited by Irenaeus less than a century after the close of the New Testament writings, according to Gustaf Aulén, a nineteenth-century Swedish theologian, this classic view "is the dominant idea of the Atonement throughout the early church period" and "the dominant idea in the New Testament."[26] Aulén offered this explanation of recapitulation in his exemplary work, *Christus Victor*:

> Its central theme is the idea of the Atonement as a Divine conflict and victory; Christ—Christus Victor—fights against and triumphs over the evil powers of the world, the "tyrants" under which mankind is in bondage and suffering, and in Him God reconciles the world to Himself.

While there are many theories of atonement within orthodoxy (e.g., Ransom Theory, Penal Substitution, Anselm's Satisfaction Theory), the theory of recapitulation offers the most definitive response to Wokeism. This isn't to say that it is the only theory that is right, as it is possible to hold multiple views of the atonement simultaneously (most theologians likely do, but Irenaeus's "Christus Victor" patently offers, in advance, both the strongest rebuttal of the tenets of Critical Theory as well as real practical solutions for many of the concerns of Wokeism, all without sacrificing the Gospel).

Within Irenaeus's writings we find an almost identical spiritual climate to the one in which we find ourselves. As we already discussed in depth, Gnosticism, as the ancient progenitor of Critical Theory, has much in common with Woke ideology. Irenaeus demonstrated that understanding the heretical views of the Gnostics wasn't enough to refute it; one must also be able to replace these deceiving views with a well-balanced theology of Christ. For Irenaeus, this began with understanding the intersection of Christ's humanity and divinity:

> He caused man (human nature) to cleave to and to become one with God. For unless man had overcome the enemy of man, the enemy would not have been legitimately vanquished. And again: unless it had been God who had freely given salvation, we could never have possessed it securely.

And unless man had been joined to God, he could never have become a partaker of the incorruptibility. For it was incumbent upon the Mediator between God and men, by His relationship to both, to bring both to friendship and concord, and present man to God, while He revealed God to man. For, in what way could we be partakers of the adoption of sons, unless we had received from Him through the Son that fellowship which refers to Himself, unless His Word, having been made flesh, had entered into communion with us?[27]

According to Irenaeus's theory of recapitulation, as a result of the sin of Adam, man lived in constant bondage to sin and death. To experience freedom from this bondage, a new Adam must be found, one who is both God and man, to vanquish the enemy and liberate humanity. Of course, this couldn't be possible, unless God "cleaved to" man in order to form a new man, Jesus Christ, the last Adam.

Combining Luke's genealogy of Jesus, Romans 5, and 1 Corinthians 15, Irenaeus constructed a vigorous argument of the parallels between Adam and Christ in order to demonstrate that Christ "summed up in Himself all nations dispersed from Adam downwards, and all languages and generations of men, together with Adam himself."[28] In this way, Christ cut through every aspect of the oppressive conditions surrounding man in order to "recapitulate," or redeem, humanity.

Irenaeus layered Paul's teaching in 1 Corinthians 15 that "since death came through a man, the resurrection of the dead comes also through a man. For as in Adam all die, so in Christ all will be made alive"[29] with Paul's admonishment to the church in Rome that "just as sin entered the world through one man, and death through sin, and in this way death came to all people, because all sinned."[30] Irenaeus also agreed with Paul that Adam was "a pattern of the one to come."[31] In Christ, the pattern was fulfilled, which Paul explained as:

But the gift is not like the trespass. For if the many died
by the trespass of the one man, how much more did God's
grace and the gift that came by the grace of the one man,
Jesus Christ, overflow to the many! Nor can the gift of God
be compared with the result of one man's sin: The judgment
followed one sin and brought condemnation, but the gift
followed many trespasses and brought justification. For if, by
the trespass of the one man, death reigned through that one
man, how much more will those who receive God's abun-
dant provision of grace and of the gift of righteousness reign
in life through the one man, Jesus Christ! Consequently,
just as one trespass resulted in condemnation for all people,
so also one righteous act resulted in justification and life
for all people. For just as through the disobedience of the
one man the many were made sinners, so also through the
obedience of the one man the many will be made righteous.
The law was brought in so that the trespass might increase.
But where sin increased, grace increased all the more, so
that, just as sin reigned in death, so also grace might reign
through righteousness to bring eternal life through Jesus
Christ our Lord.[32]

Comparing the first and last Adam, Irenaeus showed both the
similarities and distinctions between Adam and Christ. For instance,
both were created by God, without the assistance of a human father.
Additionally, both were tempted by the devil; while the first was
defeated, the second was victorious. Lastly, the first disseminated
the curse of death through the fruit of the tree, whereas the second
hung on a tree in order to dispense life to all who would receive
Him. For both Irenaeus and Paul, Adam and Christ, through the
recapitulation brought about by the death, burial, and resurrection
of Jesus, were inseparable—joined throughout history by the sinews
of redemption.

Also, inseparable in understanding *Christus Victor* for Gustaf Aulén were the incarnation and the atonement of Christ. Illuminating on the subject, he wrote:

> It is the Word of God incarnate who overcomes the tyrants which hold man in bondage; God Himself enters into the world of sin and death, that He may reconcile the world to Himself. Therefore Incarnation and Atonement stand in no sort of antithesis; rather, they belong inseparably together.[33]

With so much of modern Christianity only speaking of Jesus's death, Aulén felt that the church was being robbed of a more comprehensive victory available to it obtained by both the incarnation and the resurrection. Offering a more complete alternative, Aulén stated:

> It is evident that such a view must lay emphasis not merely on the death of Christ, but also on His victory, His triumph, His passage through death to life. According to Anselm, Christ became man primarily in order that He might die; but this isolation of the death of Christ is impossible for the patristic view. Death is, indeed, the way by which the victory is won, but the emphasis lies on the victory. Therefore the note of triumph sounds like a trumpet-call through the teaching of the early church.[34]

The "note of triumph" Aulén speaks of is at the heart of *Christus Victor*, which presents Jesus as the intersection of man and God, redeeming all of history since the Fall. As we will explore next, it is from this position of redemption, reclaiming the past, and righting every wrong that the Christus Victor view of the atonement is especially useful in answering the pessimistic existential claims of Critical Theory and Woke Christianity, with their emphasis on sins of the past, systemic oppression, and intersectionality.

Christus Victor and Wokeism

As we have seen, the common ligament between Critical Theory, and every warped theology and philosophy it has inspired, is the unified Gnostic cry of alienation. Marx spoke of estrangement due to social classes; Cone warned of the hostility of White theology; and Critical Race Theory signals an alienation brought about by White hegemony. All who aren't oppressed are oppressors standing in the way of the liberation of the people. Together, the oppressed carry forward the lonely echo of Gnosticism; that creation is one massive calamity, and existence is defined by the struggle to survive in an unsurvivable world. It's a corporeality filled with cynicism, loneliness, and dismality. This is the world the pre-existent Christ entered.

The Bible has never been shy about displaying the suffering and alienation within its pages. From Jacob to Jeremiah, to the martyrs of the church of Acts, suffering surrounds a people set apart. Arguably, the children of God have been defined by suffering and alienation. Stories, such as the life of Joseph, the captivity of the Israelites, the isolation of Elijah at Horeb,[35] and the devastation of Peter after he denied Christ for the third time remind us that alienation is not an unfamiliar condition for the believer; nor is it exclusive to the minority or oppressed. Exile, estrangement, captivity, famine, death by sword, all, like a refiner's fire, have purified and revealed the integrity and grit of the faithful. According to 1 Corinthians, such trials are "common to man;"[36] that is, alienation is part of the human experience.

Yet, the book of Hebrews helps us recall that we have a choice in how we respond to the suffering around us, as its writer honors those who, for the sake of the faith, faced unfathomable estrangement and testing:

> There were others who were tortured, refusing to be released
> so that they might gain an even better resurrection. Some
> faced jeers and flogging, and even chains and imprisonment.

They were put to death by stoning; they were sawed in two; they were killed by the sword. They went about in sheep-skins and goatskins, destitute, persecuted and mistreated— the world was not worthy of them. They wandered in deserts and mountains, living in caves and in holes in the ground. These were all commended for their faith, yet none of them received what had been promised, since God had planned something better for us so that only together with us would they be made perfect.[37]

While these accounts, conspicuously found throughout the Old and New Testaments, provide believers with untold hope and encouragement, as we, too, "face trials of many kinds,"[38] they only make up a fraction of the story of alienation that is central to the biblical narrative. At the nucleus of the Gospel are two categories of alienation, too often brushed aside, that must be addressed: alien-ation *from* God and the alienation *of* God.

One of the criticisms that progressives have against Christians is that they don't take seriously the existential reality of human suf-fering. (We'll discuss whether or not this is true and how we should handle it as Christians in the next chapter.) In actuality, it isn't that Christians don't see the suffering around them. We see the suffering that is visible, but we also see the suffering that is invisible. We see not just the abuse that's happening behind closed doors, but the concreteness of an eternal separation from God. As Jesus said, "Do not be afraid of those who kill the body but cannot kill the soul. Rather, be afraid of the One who can destroy both soul and body in hell."[39] This is the alienation that frightens us and drives much of the work of the church. Slavery or exile may be grueling, but they aren't eternal. At some point, they stop. This cannot be said, though, about the alienation of man from God.

This is one reason why the theology of *Christus Victor* offers bet-ter answers for human thrownness than does any attempt made by Critical Theory. The alienation spoken of by the Left, while tragic in its own right, is "light and momentary" compared to the weight-iness of a soul cut off from his Creator. In this way, Christus Victor warns of a more dire state of alienation than Wokeism theorizes. But unlike Hegel, Marx, or Marcuse, the Son of Man doesn't leave us to face the imminence of alienation with nothing more than an existential crisis at our disposal; rather, He enters the fray alongside us—even ahead of us!

This is why we must recognize equally both Jesus's humanity and divinity. As the triune Godhead, He willingly chose to subject Himself to the alienation of man, in order to redeem us. Jürgen Moltmann, the German theologian and author of the book *The Way of Jesus Christ*, described the willful alienation Christ chose as a "*passio activa*—a path of suffering deliberately chosen."[40] In this way, it is really Christ, God in the flesh, who is the true alien.

Who of a specific race, gender, or socioeconomic status can claim to have lost so much? Not even in a thousand lifetimes could we begin to equate the level of suffering and loss that God endured when He "emptied Himself" and became man.[41] Not only did Jesus forsake the infinite riches of heaven, but He also endured the sepa-ration from His Father on the cross, as He cried out, "Eli, Eli, lema sabachthani?" . . . "My God, my God, why have you forsaken me?"[42] Moltmann illuminates the depths of the *passio activa* even further for us:

> Yet here we have to make a clear distinction: in the surren-der of the Son the Father surrenders himself too—but not in the same way. The Son suffers His dying in this forsak-enness. The Father suffers the death of the Son. He suffers it in the infinite pain of his love for the Son. The death of the Son therefore corresponds to the pain of the Father. And when in this descent into hell the Son loses sight of the Father, then in this judgment the Father also loses sight of the Son. Here what is at stake is the divine consistency, the inner life of the Trinity. Here the self-communicating

love of the Father becomes infinite pain over the death of
the Son. Here the responding love of the Son turns into
infinite suffering over His forsakenness by the Father. What
happens on Golgotha reaches into the very depths of the
Godhead and therefore puts its impress on the trinitarian
life of God in eternity. In Christian faith the cross is always
at the centre of the Trinity, for the cross reveals the heart of
the triune God, which beats for His whole creation.[43]

It is here that we have found the true identity of the Biblical
Christ. He is our Brother, Savior, Friend, Deliverer, Redeemer, and
Lord. He is Christ the Victorious One! He navigated heaven and
earth, and even the depths of hell, to reconcile a world that was
separated from Him by the powers of sin and death. He willingly
submitted Himself to the darkest alienation imaginable and rose
victoriously, binding the powers of death and hades. As a man, He
became alienated from God Himself, and as God, He alienated
Himself from Himself, in order to offer His life as a ransom for
ours. Flesh for flesh, blood for blood. As the writer of Hebrews says:

Since the children have flesh and blood, he too shared in
their humanity so that by his death he might break the
power of him who holds the power of death—that is, the
devil—and free those who all their lives were held in slavery
by their fear of death. For surely it is not angels he helps, but
Abraham's descendants. For this reason he had to be made
like them, fully human in every way, in order that he might
become a merciful and faithful high priest in service to God,
and that he might make atonement for the sins of the people. Because he himself suffered when he was tempted, he is
able to help those who are being tempted.[44]

Thus, as Aulén presents, God is both "the Reconciler and the
Reconciled. His enmity is taken away in the very act in which He

reconciles the world unto Himself."[45] Christ the Victor is our inter-sectionality. Bridging the divide between heaven and earth, holiness and depravity, He single-handedly defeated the kingdom of darkness, conquering sin, the devil, and even the last enemy and the greatest source of alienation, death itself. Paul perfectly sums up Christ's true identity and the victory He won in his letter to the Colossians:

> The Son is the image of the invisible God, the firstborn over all creation. For in Him all things were created: things in heaven and on earth, visible and invisible, whether thrones or powers or rulers or authorities; all things have been created through him and for him. He is before all things, and in him all things hold together. And he is the head of the body, the church; he is the beginning and the firstborn from among the dead, so that in everything he might have the supremacy. For God was pleased to have all his fullness dwell in him, and through him to reconcile to himself all things, whether things on earth or things in heaven, by making peace through his blood, shed on the cross. Once you were alienated from God and were enemies in your minds because of your evil behavior. But now he has recon-ciled you by Christ's physical body through death to present you holy in his sight, without blemish and free from accu-sation—if you continue in your faith, established and firm, and do not move from the hope held out in the Gospel. This is the Gospel that you heard and that has been proclaimed to every creature under heaven, and of which I, Paul, have become a servant.[46]

Woke Christianity succeeded in finding a false messiah, because it was never looking for the real Christ. Jesus made it abundantly clear: "Ask and it will be given to you; seek and you will find." Anyone who is truly looking for the truth shall find it. Anyone searching for the Savior, rather than their own vain imaginations, will not be disappointed. Progressives in the church set out to find a Christ of their own making—one who would justify their elitist lust for unjust partiality and spiritual power—and they found him! With every new generation, progressives have lined up to continue the quest of their philosophical progenitors, wading deeper and deeper each time into the mire of heresy. Every iteration of the false messiah that they unearthed, from the original quest for the Historical Jesus, to Schleiermacher's fully human Jesus, to the "Black Messiah" of Cone's Black Liberation Theology and Critical Race Theory, is nothing but a lifeless impostor propped up by the prince of darkness to deceive God's people from finding their real hero, the God-Man, Jesus Christ.

Only the Risen and Victorious One can issue justice, forgive sins, and grant eternal life. No other has anything to offer, no life they can give. They may promise a perfect society, but they will deliver nothing but endless tyranny. As the true Messiah, Jesus traveled space and time to ransom His children from the stronghold of sin and death and established a kingdom that will endure forever! As He gave His life for ours, the veil of the temple was torn in half, symbolizing that the Spirit of God was no longer only available to the spiritual elite, but to any who would seek His face.

From the outset, the quest for the Biblical Christ was never difficult. Paul wrote in Romans 10 that there is no need to search heaven or hell looking for Him, because He says, "the word is near you; it is in your mouth and in your heart."[47] The real challenge for the church is not in finding Christ but in proclaiming His work to a hostile world; that in Christ, the Father has redeemed and reconciled all things to Himself through the victorious work of Jesus Christ. Now that we have arrived at the destination of our quest, this must become our main objective: to fortify our hearts and recover the role of the church in winning an alienated people back to Christ—no matter how hard it becomes.

CHAPTER 10

Missio Dei and the Renewal of the World

Missio Dei

"The aim always is destruction of the old world and passage to the new," wrote Eric Voegelin, undressing the Gnostic agenda in his book, *Science, Politics and Gnosticism*. Matching Jesus's description of the work of the enemy in John 10:10, Critical Theory and all of its Gnostic counterparts seek to "steal and kill and destroy,"[1] in an attempt to remake the world. This spirit of deconstruction that is pervasive throughout the Western world reinforces the need for a strong church, established in orthodoxy, capable in the spirit, and prepared to rebuild the broken walls of a just society, both figuratively and literally. While the task appears daunting, we draw encouragement from the fact that the church has done this before.

This isn't to say, though, that the work of the church is always retrospective and reminiscent. On the contrary, as Joseph Boot wrote, "Christianity as a whole . . . is future-oriented and not past-bound, God is always calling His people toward a progressive movement of covenant faithfulness in history."[2] This means that redemption and regeneration are the starting place of the Christian life—not the finish line. The real work of the church, as Boot advanced, is *missio dei*.

Missio dei, a term often appropriated by the Left, is a Latin theological term first used by Augustine, reintroduced by Thomas Aquinas, and revived during the Reformation. Augustine used the term to describe the relationship within the Trinity, in which the Father sends the Son, and the Spirit is sent by the Father and the Son:

> There you have what the Son of God has been sent for; indeed there you have what it is for the Son of God to have been sent. Everything that has taken place in time in "originated" matters which have been produced from the eternal and reduced back to the eternal, and has been designed to elicit the faith we must be purified by in order to contemplate the truth, has either been testimony to this mission or has been the actual mission of the Son of God.[3]

The reformers picked up on the covenantal language within Augustine among the Father, Son, and Spirit. They saw each member of the Trinity possessing an individual, yet collective, role in bringing about the greater purposes of God (*missio dei*). They also didn't limit these purposes to the Godhead but through the work of Christ reckoned themselves an extension of these purposes within every corner of society. According to Boot, this is what motivated the Puritans, who embraced *missio dei*, to bring revival not just to the church house, but within academics, the sciences, legal reform, and international commerce.[4] The results were an increase in prosperity and a reimagined England that stood "for the first time as a major European power and was respected throughout the world."[5]

After persecution broke out, the Puritans eventually left England for the New World, bringing with them their zeal for *missio dei*, which was largely responsible for shaping what is known as American Exceptionalism. Perhaps the best example of this is found in a sermon delivered by John Winthrop in 1630, renowned for his use of the phrase, "city on a hill," in which he declared over the new Massachusetts Bay Colony:

> Now the only way to avoid this shipwreck, and to provide for our posterity, is to follow the counsel of Micah, to do justly, to love mercy, to walk humbly with our God. For this end, we must be knit together, in this work, as one man. We must entertain each other in brotherly affection. We must be willing to abridge ourselves of our superfluities, for the supply of others' necessities. We must uphold a familiar commerce together in all meekness, gentleness, patience and liberality. We must delight in each other; make others' conditions our own; rejoice together, mourn together, labor and suffer together, always having before our eyes our commission and community in the work, as members of the same body. So shall we keep the unity of the spirit in the bond of peace. The Lord will be our God, and delight to dwell among us, as His own people, and will command a blessing upon us in all our ways, so that we shall see much more of His wisdom, power, goodness and truth, than formerly we have been acquainted with. We shall find that the God of Israel is among us, when ten of us shall be able to resist a thousand of our enemies; when He shall make us a praise and glory that men shall say of succeeding plantations, "may the Lord make it like that of New England." For we must consider that we shall be as a city upon a hill. The eyes of all people are upon us. So that if we shall deal falsely with our God in this work we have undertaken, and so cause Him to withdraw His present help from us, we shall be made a story and a by-word through the world. We shall open the mouths of enemies to speak evil of the ways of God, and all professors for God's sake. We shall shame the faces of many of God's worthy servants, and cause their prayers to

be turned into curses upon us till we be consumed out of the good land whither we are going.[6]

For Winthrop and other Puritans, the exceptionalism of New England, and eventually America, wasn't based on race or geography, but on *missio dei*. Had they found themselves in Australia or Afghanistan, it wouldn't have mattered; they likely would have made the same declarations. As Christians, they believed themselves to be participating in the work of God by organizing around the principles and precepts of God's law for a more just society.

Their commitment to *missio dei* produced the Mayflower Compact (as well as, eventually, the United States Constitution) with its dedication, for the glory of God "to enact, constitute, and frame, such just and equal Laws":[7]

> The Constitution arose from the Puritan idea of covenant. The first great document of the colonies had been the Mayflower Compact, and state after state adopted similar documents. It is interesting that the biblical book of Deuteronomy—the covenant book—was the most quoted source in political writings and speeches preceding the writing of the Constitution. There is ample reason to believe that the framers and ratifiers of the Constitution saw themselves as entering into a solemn covenant, an act of lasting and binding importance.[8]

Certainly the Founders made mistakes, but nonetheless, the Framers of our nation, nearly all of them Christian,[9] accomplished what they had set out to do: to produce the most godly and just nation in the history of civilization. While author and radio host David Barton's findings in his book *Original Intent* give us many reasons to honor and celebrate their achievement, it's most important to learn from it, especially if we want to perpetuate *missio dei* in our world today.

As Christians in the twenty-first century, to do this, we must, as Boot describes, do as the Puritans did. We will need to rid ourselves "of false humanistic assumptions about the 'neutral' areas of life and thought and see all things in the light of the good news of Christ's salvation and Lordship."[10] Perhaps only then will we have the opportunity to reverse the national damage and divisiveness caused by Critical Theory and Gnostic ideology and usher in a modern awakening to the true Christ among the citizens of this great nation.

Autonomy or Theonomy

Acting as a gateway to Progressive Christianity, the humanistic assumptions Boot warns of regarding the neutral areas of life are a major obstacle to creating a just society. Areas in which the church used to claim dominion, such as education or feeding the poor, were, in most cases, annexed by the State with little resistance from Christians. The same could be said of modern hospital systems, which were first also founded by the church.[11] Even the oversight of the institution of marriage was relinquished and subjected to state definitions and legislation, reducing the church's influence to mostly ceremonial rather than authoritative. Christians' acquiescence of social responsibility to establishments outside the church's jurisdiction wasn't always the case.

Joseph Boot explains that a central aspect to early American Christianity was that "Christians were responsible to God for the care and compassion they showed to others. Neighbour love ... was a rudimentary requirement for believers."[12] While some might be concerned that this sounds like a theocracy, it's not; as Boot explains, it's either "autonomy or theonomy—selflaw or God's law."[13]

As not all may be familiar with the term, a theonomy is a people governed by God's law, whereas a theocracy is a government led by a state-sponsored religious group. As Christians, we should all desire to live within a theonomous community in which God's rule and reign are welcomed within every corner of civil and moral law. Boot describes the compassionate attitude this took on within Puritan communities:

> The Puritans did not contract this task [compassion] out to the state and its welfare programs. Ryken explains that "The Puritans did not share the confidence of our century that social cohesion depends on governmental structures. Rather they understood the crucial role played by the spirit of community." A public spirit was required of all believers, so a failure to care for social needs was believed to hold negative consequences.... Help for those in need went well beyond giving alms to the poor. They funded students through university. They bought books and Bibles for those who could not afford them. They helped people find employment and start businesses. They cared for orphans, widows, and the destitute.[14]

It's important to note, that a theonomy and a democratic republic aren't mutually exclusive. Rather than a form of government, a theonomy guides those elected as they consider how their policies and ordinances align with the truth of God's Word. Without this, justice, which can only be found within God's Law, will remain fleeting. Addressing humanistic notions at a community level alone will never be enough, though, to revive justice, if we don't also turn our attention to the individual assumptions that make up the collective ethos regarding neutral areas common within the Christian psyche. To convince ourselves that certain areas of our life, from our sexuality to our spending habits, somehow don't fall under the jurisdiction of the Lordship of Jesus—that in these areas we are able to make our own rules—is the height of arrogance. As Christians, we willingly submit ourselves to His total Lordship. He is Lord over all, not just a part.

While Wokeism may give man a wide radius of personal autonomy, that is, to apply his own morals toward any given situation,

Christianity does not. The Lordship of Jesus invites us to bow the knee in every area of our lives. Leaving nothing belonging to us alone, nor any area that is outside of His authority—this is commitment to *missio dei*.

According to Boot, the Puritan's commitment to *missio dei* "could not tolerate the notion that the Christian Faith could be limited to a vertical relationship between a person and God by individual regeneration, especially when used as a way of escaping from the responsibility of applying God's word to all things in the common life of mankind; such a view was seen as a denial of the incarnation."[15] This means, if we model it, that our Christianity must extend beyond our personal faith, in such a way that allows Christ to reign over every sphere of society. Whether they know it or not, this is what the world is longing for; as the psalmist writes, "The Lord reigns, let the earth be glad; let the distant shores rejoice" (Ps 97:1 NIV). If these were the demands of an evil dictator, this wouldn't seem very attractive, but since it is the call of our benevolent Savior God, Jesus Christ, we can rest assured that His way is always better than our own.

Applying *Missio Dei*

If we are to convince the Left to abandon their Woke Jesus and return once again to a biblical worldview, then our embrace of *missio dei* must be more than theological; it must also be practical. This means that as we wait for the return of the Lord Jesus, our involvement in bringing heaven to earth must consist of more than riling ourselves up listening to conservative media. While there is certainly nothing wrong with supporting conservative media (and I think that we should support outlets such as Fox News and Newsmax), our viewership cannot be misconstrued within our own hearts as activism. Simply being informed on the issues isn't enough. Too many have been consumed with watching the media, only to become frustrated and disenchanted with society.[16] Their knowledge of the situation grows, but it scarcely leads to activism. When it does, actions seldom involve faith. Conservatism may be promoted, but this is not the same as *missio dei*.

Additionally, it's important that as Christians we become known by what we are for, more than by what we are against. One would be hard pressed to read the book of Acts and only leave with a contrarian theology of the church, of what it opposes, rather than a celebratory and liberating theology of the cross. The conservative movement, though, in too many instances, has become an "anti-party." We speak more of being anti-vaccines, anti-CRT, anti-BLM, and anti-socialism, than of being pro-life, pro-justice, pro-God, pro-free market, and pro-church. And while we should be against all of these things, this "anti" stance, especially among the previous generation of Republicans, gives the impression that conservativism isn't doing all that much.

Wokeism, on the other hand, is appealing, especially to Millennials and Gen Zs, because an allegiance to it appears to be accomplishing something or participating in a real way toward solving problems. Protests, boycotts, and even looting and rioting, are upheld by many to be viable methods of driving social change and are attractive to those with a bent toward activism. Rarely, though, are Woke actions considered in light of the scriptures. As long as biblically sounding generic terminology can define and justify each action (e.g., "love" and "justice"), then hardly ever are Woke behaviors held accountable to any sort of genuine Christian standard. If they were, then we would quickly see that Wokeism has only led to increased racial tension, unbalanced scales of mob justice, sexual libertinism, and a complete lack of personal responsibility. None of these traits aligns with biblical ideology and none will ever help contribute to a more just society. In the end, Wokeism only promotes evil and injustice, but what else should we expect from an ideology that has its roots in one of the most heartless and malevolent movements to ever befall the Western world?

America: Privileged and Ill-Informed

Over the last 100 years, this planet has faced some of the most oppressive and tyrannical regimes in the annals of world history. The twentieth century alone gave us monsters like Adolf Hitler and Mao Zedong, plus countless ruthless and unjust autocrats, like the Soviet Union's Vladimir Lenin and Joseph Stalin. That's not even mentioning the lesser-known dictators of Latin America and Africa: Manuel Antonio Noriega (Panama); Fidel Castro (Cuba); Idi Amin (Uganda); Robert Mugabe (Zimbabwe); or Omar Hassan Ahmad Al-Bashir (Sudan). The Communist states alone are responsible for as many as 100 million deaths, yet privileged, and often ill-informed, Wokeists try to pretend that the sins of the United States are the gravest in world history.

Due in part to government-endorsed educational propaganda,[17] like the 1619 Project, a new generation of Americans are being indoctrinated with the idea that the Judeo-Christian values that shaped this nation are to blame for everything from rape culture to unarmed Black men being gunned down by police officers in the streets.

For instance, Arwa Mahdawi, a columnist for *The Guardian*, jabbed at Lady Liberty, stating, "Rape culture is as American as apple pie."[18] Likewise, Woke journalist and comic book author Ta-Nehisi Coates claimed in an editorial for *The Atlantic* that the "heritage and legacy" of America is the "shackling of black bodies."[19]

Like every nation, the United States of America has a tarnished record of grievances and historical atrocities that are easy to criticize, but these hardly define her. Nodding their hat to James Cone, that sin is a "community concept"[20] instead of an individualistic act, Wokeists indict the nation collectively, based on the actions of a few rather than the accomplishments of the many. Forgotten are America's unprecedented contributions to global freedom and personal liberty throughout the years, such as the introduction of the Declaration of Independence and the Bill of Rights, the abolition of slavery, the welcoming of countless millions of legal immigrants as well as religious and political refugees, granting women equal voting rights, vanquishing the Nazis and freeing Europe, and the Civil Rights Act of 1964.

For the Woke, these accomplishments will never be enough. As long as a single injustice exists, America (and the Christian faith) will be judged racist, misogynistic, and bigoted. Under this standard, progress is always fleeting, because absent of the Kingdom of God, sin will always surface in a community of people. The irony, of course, is that behind many of these accusations of injustice are well-funded tenured professors, wealthy progressive pastors, and cynical college students, all of whom have benefited greatly from America's free society and capitalist system. Based on this, if America's present legacy is anything, it's a legacy of ingratitude.

As a false religion, Wokeism promotes what Scott David Allen, author of *Why Social Justice Is Not Biblical Justice*, called "a culture of hatred, division, a false sense of moral superiority and a false understanding of justice. A culture where truth is replaced by power, and gratitude by ingratitude."[21] As a natural response to a loss of perspective, ingratitude is the corresponding state embraced by those who have lost sight of the undeservedness of God's grace. Though this spirit of entitlement grips our nation, we aren't the first to lose our way in its grasp.

Remembrance and Entitlement

Delivered from 400 years of enslavement at the hands of the Egyptians, the Israelites knew a little something about injustice. In Deuteronomy 8, the Lord gave Moses instructions to share with the people of Israel a way to protect their hearts against entitlement, by observing His commands and retaining the knowledge of their past liberation:

When you have eaten and are satisfied, praise the Lord your
God for the good land he has given you. Be careful that
you do not forget the Lord your God, failing to observe his
commands, his laws and his decrees that I am giving you
this day. Otherwise, when you eat and are satisfied, when
you build fine houses and settle down, and when your herds
and flocks grow large and your silver and gold increase and
all you have is multiplied, then your heart will become proud
and you will forget the Lord your God, who brought you
out of Egypt, out of the land of slavery. He led you through
the vast and dreadful wilderness, that thirsty and waterless
land, with its venomous snakes and scorpions. He brought
you water out of hard rock. He gave you manna to eat in the
wilderness, something your ancestors had never known, to
humble and test you so that in the end it might go well with
you. You may say to yourself, "My power and the strength of
my hands have produced this wealth for me." But remember
the Lord your God, for it is he who gives you the ability
to produce wealth, and so confirms his covenant, which he
swore to your ancestors, as it is today. If you ever forget the
Lord your God and follow other gods and worship and bow
down to them, I testify against you today that you will surely
be destroyed.[22]

As the Israelites entered the promised land and enjoyed the prosperity that accompanied liberation, God wanted to ensure that they
wouldn't forget how they got there and "become proud." If they did,
the stakes were clear: they would "surely be destroyed." God's remedy to prevent this was simple: they were to walk in remembrance.

Regarding God's commands and promises, the Israelites were
told to keep them "on your hearts" and to "impress them on your
children. Talk about them when you sit at home and when you walk
along the road, when you lie down and when you get up. . . . Write
them on the doorframes of your houses and on your gates."[23] God

knew that through a constant remembrance, the people of God could ward off the cancer of entitlement. With brilliant foresight, God anticipated the future generations that wouldn't understand:

> In the future, when your son asks you, "What is the mean-
> ing of the stipulations, decrees and laws the Lord our God
> has commanded you?" tell him: "We were slaves of Pharaoh
> in Egypt, but the Lord brought us out of Egypt with a
> mighty hand. Before our eyes the Lord sent signs and
> wonders—great and terrible—on Egypt and Pharaoh and
> his whole household. But he brought us out from there to
> bring us in and give us the land he promised on oath to our
> ancestors. The Lord commanded us to obey all these decrees
> and to fear the Lord our God, so that we might always
> prosper and be kept alive, as is the case today. And if we are
> careful to obey all this law before the Lord our God, as he
> has commanded us, that will be our righteousness.'24

This perhaps is the greatest sin of the Woke; they have forgotten that the Lord delivered us, not only from the physical bondage of slavery, but also from the spiritual bondage of sin and death. Like Israel, they have found fault with the Lord, blaming Him for the trials of life rather than recognizing how their own actions and the sins of a fallen world have contributed to their pain and alienation.

The Apostle Paul combated a similar entitlement mentality in the first-century church in Corinth. He wrote:

> What do you have that you did not receive? And if you
> did receive it, why do you boast as though you did not?
> Already you have all you want! Already you have become
> rich! You have begun to reign—and that without us! How
> I wish that you really had begun to reign so that we also
> might reign with you! For it seems to me that God has
> put us apostles on display at the end of the procession, like

those condemned to die in the arena. We have been made a spectacle to the whole universe, to angels as well as to human beings. We are fools for Christ, but you are so wise in Christ! We are weak, but you are strong! You are honored, we are dishonored! To this very hour we go hungry and thirsty, we are in rags, we are brutally treated, we are homeless. We work hard with our own hands. When we are cursed, we bless; when we are persecuted, we endure it; when we are slandered, we answer kindly. We have become the scum of the earth, the garbage of the world—right up to this moment.[25]

In the face of impossible circumstances, Paul exhibited a spiritual resiliency that refused to quit. With his focus on the things of heaven, the great apostle was willing to confront the challenges of ministry without losing heart—even if such circumstances led to his own condemnation. Such selflessness is at the center of *missio dei* and offers us a glimpse at the most important and final distinction between Wokeism and Biblical Christianity.

Suffering for Christ

Paul, more than anyone else besides Christ, understood that following the plan and purposes of the Father would ultimately lead to suffering. Throughout his ministry, the apostle to the Gentiles, who forewarned "everyone who wants to live a godly life in Christ Jesus will be persecuted,"[26] suffered:

- Imprisoned on multiple occasions
- Scourged five different times with "forty lashes minus one"
- Three beatings with a rod
- Pelted with stones
- Shipwrecked three different times
- Danger from natural disasters and from the hands of men

- Countless sleepless nights
- Hunger and thirst
- Exposed to the elements
- Countless other ailments and adversities[27]

Yet, in all of these things, he was full of faith and overflowing with joy. For Paul, suffering wasn't a curse, nor did he view himself as powerless against his oppressors. In his mind, he considered everything he endured at the hands of sinful men a "loss for the sake of Christ."[28] Said another way, Paul's sufferings were proof that he was living out *missio dei*.

Encased in human agony, but uplifted by spiritual ecstasy, Paul wrote:

> I want to know Christ—yes, to know the power of his
> resurrection and participation in his sufferings, becoming
> like him in his death, and so, somehow, attaining to the
> resurrection from the dead. Not that I have already obtained
> all this, or have already arrived at my goal, but I press on
> to take hold of that for which Christ Jesus took hold of
> me. Brothers and sisters, I do not consider myself yet to
> have taken hold of it. But one thing I do: Forgetting what
> is behind and straining toward what is ahead, I press on
> toward the goal to win the prize for which God has called
> me heavenward in Christ Jesus.[29]

Like Paul, the Apostle Peter also embraced suffering for the sake of the Gospel as part of God's mission for his life. The fisherman-turned-disciple wrote to the scattered believers throughout Asia Minor in his first letter, encouraging them as they faced the coming persecution:

> Therefore, since Christ suffered in his body, arm yourselves
> also with the same attitude, because whoever suffers in the

body is done with sin. As a result, they do not live the rest of their earthly lives for evil human desires, but rather for the will of God. For you have spent enough time in the past doing what pagans choose to do—living in debauchery, lust, drunkenness, orgies, carousing and detestable idolatry. They are surprised that you do not join them in their reckless, wild living, and they heap abuse on you. But they will have to give account to him who is ready to judge the living and the dead. For this is the reason the Gospel was preached even to those who are now dead, so that they might be judged according to human standards in regard to the body, but live according to God in regard to the spirit.[30]

Herein we find the final distinction between Wokeism and Biblical Christianity: Wokeism robs the believer of the ability to suffer for the sake of Christ. Within Wokeism, all suffering is derived from external factors, such as skin color, country of origin, or socioeconomic class. As such, stripped of the blessing of offering their lives unto God, those who subscribe to Woke ideology can only ever suffer for their own sake.

In Christian suffering, however, we selflessly sacrifice our lives and bodies for the sake of Christ. Wokeism, on the other hand, takes an act that is intended to be consecrated by selflessness and desecrates it with ego, pride, and arrogance. Far from living out the words of John the Baptist, that "He must become greater; I must become less,"[31] Progressive Christians take the attention off of Christ until all eyes are on them, and receive, as Jesus says, "their reward in full."[32]

On the contrary, as Christians, we delight in God's call on our life and "consider it pure joy . . . whenever [we] face trials of many kinds."[33] We gladly turn the other cheek[34] when insults and ridicule come our way. When suffering, we refuse to see our hardships as directed toward ourselves, because we remember our Savior's words: "If the world hates you, keep in mind that it hated me first."[35] This allows us to find comfort in the fact that we are not alone, nor alienated, as the God-Man, Jesus Christ, shared in our humanity and gave His life as a ransom for our sins. This means that when persecution and oppression come against us, we can rejoice, knowing that we are living out *missio dei* to the glory of the true and eternal one, Jesus Christ.

Playing the Long Game

If we have learned anything about Critical Theorists, especially Socialists and Communists, it's that they are willing to play the long game. Dedicated to their cynical worldview, the descendants of Marxist and Hegelian thought seem quite content to implement their strategy toward societal deconstruction over the span of decades. From Russia's drawn-out relationship with Syria and Turkey, to China's "strategic ambitions to replace the U.S. as leader of the global order,"[36] there is no shortage of examples of Critical Theory patiently at work within our borders and on a world scale.

The methodology of the Radical Left playing out in America today is described by W. Cleon Skousen, author of *The Naked Communist*, as a "process of corruption." Unpacking this further, he wrote:

> Conquering a nation typically comes about in one of two ways. The first is to attack it militarily and compel the people to obedience. The second is to corrupt the institutions that keep the people unified, and raise up leaders who promise to stabilize the chaos, establish order and return a sense of security. America was too strong to conquer militarily, so the second process was undertaken, the process of corruption.[37]

Few institutions are responsible for unifying the nation more than the church. As such, it's imperative, both spiritually for the sake of the lost and geo-politically for the sake of global freedom, that orthodox Christianity prove true. For these reasons, every Christian should take seriously their role in pushing back the darkness of Wokeism and Critical Theory in all of its forms. For those requiring some practical examples of how to get started, here are some ideas:

1. **Don't attend a Woke Church.** If you consistently see evidence that your pastor, elders, or other church leaders are promoting Critical Race Theory, Wokeism, or Critical Theory, it's time to find a new church. If you aren't sure, ask questions. Ask your leaders what they know about Critical Race Theory, whether they believe the Bible is truly the inerrant Word of God, and where they stand on same-sex marriage. Make your case clear, but remember, you don't have to argue. If you find that your church leaders have abandoned a biblical worldview, vote with your feet and tithe check, and move on.

2. **Know what your child is being taught in school.** If you have a child in the public school system, it's crucial that you take the time to research what they are being taught. This should include asking about any lessons on Critical Race Theory; Social and Emotional Learning; and Diversity, Equity, and Inclusion instruction. You should also ask whether the school has a policy on pornographic material in the classrooms and school library. Many parents are finding that distorted views of sexuality and gender are being introduced to their children through graphic books in circulation within the school's library. If you don't like what you hear, consider enrolling your child in a private Christian school or, if it's an option, homeschooling your child. Teaching your child to walk with the Lord will become increasingly more difficult if they are constantly bombarded with contrarian materials.

3. **Support a conservative candidate, or run for office.** Representation by godly men and women in our government is vital to maintaining religious freedom. As a result of the "red wave" around the country, most communities now

have active conservative groups already working within their region. Meet with these leaders, and discuss ways that you can support their efforts.

4. **Serve in a helps ministry.** By serving in a helps ministry (e.g., feeding program, single mother or elderly care, teen mentoring, pregnancy center), you are able to simultaneously be the hands and feet of Jesus while also sharing a biblical worldview with other volunteers and those whom you're serving. It's also a great way to remind yourself of the practical ministry of the Gospel.

5. **Plant yourself in a local church.** Christian accountability is one of the most important aspects of discipleship. As believers, we are not exempt from the regular fellowship and accountability that a local church can provide. Our regular time, service, attendance, and support of a local church will strengthen our own faith and help further the Gospel. This is one of the most important commitments in your life that you can make.

The Battle Is Far from Over

As I've spent the last several years touring the country and warning of the dangers of the "Christian Left," I've heard from countless Christians who have told me that they don't like to hear the negativity about how the Left is rewriting scripture and reframing the church. "I just want to get back to talking about Jesus," they say. While I am truly empathetic to this position, I must point out that this perspective is at least partially to blame for how we got here in the first place.

In the book of Ephesians, the Apostle Paul gives us fatherly wisdom, "Therefore each of you must put off falsehood and speak truthfully to your neighbor, for we are all members of one body. 'In your anger do not sin': Do not let the sun go down while you are still angry, and do not give the devil a foothold."[38] To illustrate why this work is so important, I'd like to point out several truths contained in Paul's words.

First, Paul charges us to "put off falsehood" and "speak truthfully." To do so requires two things: We must know the truth, and we must be willing to tell someone what it is. I don't believe that Paul is lobbying for pouncing on complete strangers to tell them what's wrong with their lives. The insinuation here is that these individuals are "neighbors;" people we know. Far from a mind-bending revelation, this simple concept alone, speaking truth to those closest to us, would likely correct the course of many who are wayward within the church today.

Second, Paul reminds us that as we speak to one another we should remember that we are neighbors and more specifically, members of one body. This mind-set frames our conversations in love and helps us overcome what I've called the "deadly cycle of worry, anger, and apathy."[39] Keep in mind, truth without love is only judgment. By keeping love as the motivation for the reason we speak the truth, many errors can be avoided.

Third, Paul gives us this interesting nugget, to never "let the sun go down while we are still angry." This advice is typically only given to married couples regarding how to end an argument before bedtime, but I would argue that we've missed what Paul is trying to tell us. The Amplified Bible translation offers us a more in-depth look at the meaning behind Paul's words. It reads, "Be angry [at sin—at immorality, at injustice, at ungodly behavior], yet do not sin; do not let your anger [cause you shame, nor allow it to] last until the sun goes down."

Based on this translation, it appears that Paul is actually telling us that we need to get a little fired up and angry at injustice and immorality, but that we must do so in a way that doesn't control us. A man whose anger controls him will toss and turn all night wrought with frustration and worry. On the other hand, a man in control of his anger he can set his righteous indignation down for the night and rest peacefully, knowing that ultimately God is his defender. This is how we prevent the devil from gaining a foothold.

I know all too well that the topics in this book can be infuriating and deeply concerning for Christians. All of us have loved ones who have likely been affected by the Wokeist agenda, and perhaps even some who have de-converted from the faith over many of these issues. On a personal level, know that I understand more than I would like to admit, the heartache of watching those you love as they are lured away by the siren song of the Social Justice movement. I want to leave you with this:

- Don't ignore the problems within the church.
- Grow in the truth of God's Word, and expand your understanding of solid orthodox theology.
- Refuse to allow your anger at the enemy to dilute your love for people.
- Be bold in sharing your faith with others.
- Remember that grace and truth are the keys to avoiding every error.
- Most importantly, don't give up the fight—the church's best days are still ahead.

Notes

Introduction

1. Irenaeus of Lyons, *Against Heresies*, Ex Fontibus Co., 2010, pp. 27–28.
2. The author has benefited personally from the works of Voddie Baucham, Dr. Owen Strachan, and James Lindsay.
3. https://www.faithwire.com/2017/05/17/percentage-of-americans -who-believe-bible-is-literal-word-of-god-plunges-and-gallup -reveals-the-consequences/.
4. Ibid.
5. Genesis 3:1 NIV.
6. 1 John 2:19 NIV.
7. Immanuel Kant, *Religion within the Boundaries of Mere Reason*, Cambridge University Press, 2018, p. 98.
8. Ibid., p. 157.
9. "Could Kant's Jesus be God?" https://philarchive.org/archive/ PALCKJ.
10. Kant, *Religion within the Boundaries of Mere Reason*, p. 97.
11. That is, "by Grace through Faith."
12. Kant, *Religion within the Boundaries of Mere Reason*, p. 151.
13. "Could Kant's Jesus be God?"
14. Ibid.
15. https://www.washingtonpost.com/posteverything/wp/2014/12/18/ did-historical-jesus-exist-the-traditional-evidence-doesnt-hold-up/.
16. Kant, *Religion within the Boundaries of Mere Reason*, p. 115.

Chapter 1

1. https://www.frc.org/updatearticle/20201204/woke-denomination.
2. Ibid.
3. Ibid.
4. Ibid.
5. https://www.thelmx.org/.
6. Ibid.
7. Eric Mason, *Woke Church*, Moody Publishers, 2018, p. 25.
8. Also referred to as simply the "Frankfurt School."
9. https://www.yalelawjournal.org/essay/police-reform-and-the
   -dismantling-of-legal-estrangement.
10. https://www.heritage.org/education/commentary/tackle-critical
    -theory-the-k-12-classroom-start-colleges-education.
11. Ibid.
12. Owen Strachan, *Christianity and Wokeness*, Salem Books, 2021, p. 45.
13. James H. Cone, *A Black Theology of Liberation, Fortieth Anniversary Edition*, Orbis Books, 2020, p. 94.
14. https://capstonereport.com/2021/01/21/ed-litton-is-woke-and-will
    -destroy-the-sbc/35450/.
15. https://onenewsnow.com/church/2021/03/12/on-moores-departure
    -sbc-not-woke-enough-for-her.
16. https://www.christianitytoday.com/scot-mcknight/2020/october/
    jesus-refugee.html.
17. https://reboot4life.wordpress.com/2014/08/14/that-time-when
    -jesus-started-a-riot/.
18. https://www.theguardian.com/commentisfree/belief/2012/apr/20/
    was-jesus-gay-probably.
19. Herbert Marcuse (1898–1979) was a German American philosopher, activist, and member of the Frankfurt School of Critical Theory. Marcuse criticized capitalism, advocated for Marxist ideals, and was one of the most influential and radical Critical Theorists of his day.
20. https://www.youtube.com/watch?v=EnmlGOVETio.
21. https://www.youtube.com/watch?v=OYfMgf1P9rc.
22. https://www.michaelwear.com/.
23. https://www.youtube.com/watch?v=oQUIZgpxRkI.
24. Helen Pluckrose and James Lindsay, *Cynical Theories*, Pitchstone Publishing, 2020, pp. 22–23.

25. https://www.churchtimes.co.uk/articles/2018/15-june/features/
features/heresy-holiness-and-oprah-rob-bell-interviewed.
26. http://dougpagitt.com/.
27. https://www.votecommongood.com/.
28. https://www.votecommongood.com/what-and-why/.
29. 1 Chronicles 12:32 NIV.
30. Galatians 6:1 NIV.
31. Matthew 23:15 NIV.
32. https://twitter.com/michaelgungor/status/312078430457954305.
33. Georg Wilhem Friedrich Hegel, *Phenomenology of Spirit*, Oxford
University Press, 1977, p. 487.
34. Ibid., p. 492.
35. Ibid., p. 478.
36. https://sites.evergreen.edu/arunchandra/wp-content/uploads/sites/
395/2018/07/tolerance.pdf.
37. Ibid.
38. For more on this topic, see my previous book, *The Christian
Left: How Liberal Thought Has Hijacked the Church*, Lucas Miles,
Broadstreet Publishing Group, 2021.
39. https://plato.stanford.edu/entries/hegel-dialectics/#HegeDescHis
DialMeth.
40. A theory that holds that authority is found through personal
knowledge.
41. https://newdiscourses.com/2021/05/hegel-wokeness-and-the
-dialectical-faith-of-leftism/.
42. https://www.marxists.org/subject/dialectics/marx-engels/capital
-afterward.htm.
43. Ibid.
44. Ibid.
45. Mohler himself has been accused of being a "double agent" of the
Christian Left. https://capstonereport.com/2021/01/02/former
-sbts-faculty-prof-al-mohler-is-double-agent/.
46. https://albertmohler.com/2017/01/03/briefing-01-03-17.
47. https://pulpitandpen.org/2020/09/01/blm-benediction-priest
-leads-catholics-through-mass-with-worlds-wokest-prayer/.
48. Philip J. Lee, *Against the Protestant Gnostics*, Oxford University
Press, 1987.
49. Ibid.

50. R. T. Allen, "Flew, Marx and Gnosticism," *Philosophy* 68, no. 263, 1993, pp. 94–98. JSTOR, www.jstor.org/stable/3751068.
51. Eric Voegelin, *Science, Politics, & Gnosticism*, p. 82.
52. Ibid, p. 82–83.
53. 2 Corinthians 5:7 NIV.
54. https://www.catholicworldreport.com/2021/01/31/the-gnostic-heresys-political-successors/.
55. Ibid.
56. Ibid.
57. Ibid.
58. Ibid.
59. Samuel N. C. Lieu, *Manichaeism in the Later Roman Empire and Medieval China: A Historical Survey*, 1999, p. 6.
60. Ibid., p. 10.
61. Genesis 2:7 NIV.
62. Lieu, *Manichaeism in the Later Roman Empire and Medieval China*, p. 12.
63. https://en.wikipedia.org/wiki/.Manichaeism#cite_note-SNC_Lieu-25.
64. Ephesians 5:14b.

Chapter 2

1. Joseph F. Girzone, *A Portrait of Jesus*, Doubleday, 1998, p. 71.
2. Apollinarius was a heretical Bishop of Laodicea in 362 AD. His teachings on Jesus rejected the humanity of Christ.
3. Nestorius, appointed Patriarch of Constantinople in 428 AD, emphasized a heretical view that separated Christ into two persons, human and divine, rather than one man, who was fully human and fully God.
4. G. K. Chesterton, *The Everlasting Man*, 2012, p. 201.
5. Although Reimarus was born prior to Kant, his "Fragments" on the life of Christ weren't published until after his death in 1774, because they were too controversial to release during his lifetime. Kant's most important works weren't published until after this, but he had become an important theorist and a published writer as early as the mid-1750s, thus arguably playing a small part for the elder thinker Reimarus's work to be received.
6. Albert Schweitzer, *The Quest of the Historical Jesus*, A. and C. Black, 1911.

7. Craig S. Keener, *The Historical Jesus of the Gospels*, p. 4.
8. Ibid., p. 3.
9. Ibid. p. 6.
10. Ibid. p. 6.
11. Schweitzer, *The Quest of the Historical Jesus*, p. 7.
12. Ibid., p. 13.
13. Ibid., p. 15.
14. Ibid., p. 15.
15. Schweitzer, *The Quest of the Historical Jesus*, p. 4.
16. Ibid.
17. Gotthold Ephraim Lessing, Charles Voysey, Hermann Samuel Reimarus, *Fragments from Reimarus: Consisting of Brief Critical Remarks on the Object of Jesus and His Disciples as Seen in the New Testament*, Andesite Press, 1879, pp. 46–47.
18. Keener, *The Historical Jesus of the Gospels*, p. 4.
19. https://www.huffpost.com/entry/jesus-the-first-transgend_b_10006134.
20. https://www.masonrytoday.com/index.php?new_month=08&new_day=25&new_year=2018.
21. Schweitzer, *The Quest of the Historical Jesus*, p. 38.
22. Ibid.
23. Heinrich Paulus 1761–1851.
24. Schweitzer, *The Quest of the Historical Jesus*, p. 48.
25. Ibid., p. 53.
26. Ibid., p. 54.
27. John Dominic Crossan, *The Historical Jesus: The Life of a Mediterranean Jewish Peasant*, Harper Collins, 1992, p. xxviii.
28. Schweitzer, *The Quest of the Historical Jesus*, p. 399.
29. Jacob Neusner, "Who Needs 'The Historical Jesus'? An Essay-Review," *Bulletin for Biblical Research* 4, Penn State University Press, 1994, pp. 113–26, JSTOR, http://www.jstor.org/stable/26422106.
30. Ibid.
31. Ibid.
32. 2 Timothy 3:16-17 NIV.
33. Schweitzer, *The Quest of the Historical Jesus*, p. 401.
34. List adapted from https://www.crosswalk.com/blogs/debbie-mc daniel/50-names-of-jesus-who-the-bible-says-christ-is.html.
35. https://www.firstthings.com/article/2021/10/the-Historical-adam.
36. Ibid.

37. https://youtu.be/t563ah5i7iw.

38. https://www.nbcnews.com/news/world/dead-sea-scrolls-discover ies-are-first-ancient-bible-texts-be-n1261182.

39. The author agrees with Goodacre and holds to the Farrer Hypothesis, which proposes the Markan priority, that Luke had access to Mark and that Matthew likely had access to both Mark and Luke. Thus eradicating the need for Q or any other missing lost text.

40. Mark Goodacre, *The Case Against Q*, Trinity Press, 2002, p. 3.

41. Keener, *The Historical Jesus of the Gospels*, p. 61.

42. Bart D. Ehrman, *Jesus: Apocalyptic Prophet of the New Millennium*, Oxford University Press, 1999, p. 81.

43. Ibid., p. 82.

44. https://www.abc.net.au/religion/how-god-became-jesus-bart-eh rman-gets-it-wrong-again/10099302.

45. Robert Funk, Arthur Dewey, and the Jesus Seminar, *The Gospel of Jesus*, Polebridge Press, 2015, p. xii.

46. Ibid.

47. Keener, *The Historical Jesus of the Gospels*, p. 15.

48. Ibid., p. 5.

49. Ibid., p. 7.

50. https://youtu.be/t563ah5i7iw.

51. C. S. Lewis, *Mere Christianity*, First Touchstone Edition, 1996, p. 56.

Chapter 3

1. https://www.thecollegefix.com/theology-professor-defends-her -dear-god-please-help-me-to-hate-White-people-prayer/.

2. James H. Cone, *A Black Theology of Liberation*, Orbis Books, 1990, p. 8.

3. Ibid.

4. Ibid., p. 36.

5. Ibid., 115.

6. Ibid., p. 10.

7. Ibid., p. 91.

8. 1 John 2:2 NIV.

9. Cone, *A Black Theology of Liberation*, p. 123.

10. Karl Barth sought to elevate the supremacy of Christ by discon- necting Him from the written word of a book that was often only

collecting dust on a shelf. His desire wasn't to downgrade scripture but to elevate Jesus. Barth believed that only when the Bible was being preached could it be referred to as "the Word of God."

11. Cone, *A Black Theology of Liberation*, p. 41.
12. Ibid., p. 116.
13. Ibid.
14. Ibid., p. 120.
15. Ibid., p. 127.
16. Ibid., p. 40.
17. Ibid., p. 26.
18. Ibid., p. 48.
19. Ibid., p. 95.
20. Cone, *A Black Theology of Liberation*, p. 40.
21. Some scholars believe Gilgamesh is synonymous with the biblical figure Nimrod, though this is debated.
22. Also known as Humbaba. Associated with the Hebrew Jehovah.
23. https://christianhistoryinstitute.org/magazine/article/jesus-was -not-a-White-man.
24. Cone, *A Black Theology of Liberation*, p. 21.
25. Galatians 3:28 NIV.
26. Acts 2:5 NIV.
27. Revelation 7:9 NIV.
28. Susannah Heschel, *The Aryan Jesus*, Princeton University Press, 2008, p. 1.
29. Ibid., p. 26.
30. Ibid., p. 27.
31. Ibid., p. 49.
32. Ibid., p. 38.
33. Ibid., p. 40.
34. Ibid., p. 48.
35. *Volk* is the German word for "people," specifically related to the German ethnicity.
36. George L. Mosse, *The Crisis of German Ideology*, Grosset and Dunlap, 1964, pp. 24–25.
37. https://www.rollingstone.com/culture/culture-features/capitol -christian-right-trump-1121236/.
38. https://www.washingtonpost.com/religion/2021/07/06/capitol -insurrection-trump-christian-nationalism-shaman/.

39. https://www.theatlantic.com/politics/archive/2021/01/evangelicals
    -catholics-jericho-march-capitol/617591/.
40. https://www.npr.org/2021/01/19/958159202/militant-christian
    -nationalists-remain-a-potent-force.
41. https://religionnews.com/2021/07/27/police-officer-calls-january
    -6-insurrectionists-terrorists-who-perceived-themselves-to-be
    -christians/.
42. https://time.com/6052051/anti-democratic-threat-christian
    -nationalism/.
43. https://www.cfr.org/event/rise-christian-nationalism.
44. Ibid.
45. https://reformationcharlotte.org/2020/06/05/southern-baptist
    -leader-ed-stetzer-marches-in-antifa-Black-lives-matter-protest
    -in-chicago/.
46. https://www.michaelwear.com/publicsquarestrategies.
47. https://www.christiansandthevaccine.com/about.
48. https://www.washingtonpost.com/religion/2020/10/02/new
    -evangelical-leaders-support-biden/.
49. https://rmnetwork.org/.
50. https://www.outkick.com/michael-moore-christians-taliban
    -afghanistan-kabul/.
51. https://www.ama-assn.org/delivering-care/public-health/5-reasons
    -why-religious-services-pose-high-risk-covid-19-spread.
52. https://encyclopedia.ushmm.org/content/en/article/the-boycott-of
    -jewish-businesses.
53. https://perspectives.ushmm.org/item/propaganda-poster-jews-are
    -lice-they-cause-typhus.
54. https://www.cfr.org/event/rise-christian-nationalism.
55. Ibid.
56. Adolf Hitler, *Table Talk*, Enigma Books, 2000, p. 62.
57. Ibid., p. 722.
58. bid., p. 76.
59. https://www.cfr.org/event/rise-christian-nationalism.
60. Hitler, *Table Talk*, p. 145.
61. Cone, *A Black Theology of Liberation*, p. 65.

Chapter 4

1. https://www.pbs.org/wgbh/americanexperience/features/billy
   -graham-tale-two-preachers/.

2. Jeremiah 8:20 NIV.
3. Derrick Bell, *And We Are Not Saved*, Basic Books, 1989, p. 16.
4. Ibid., pp. 16, 17.
5. Ibid., p. 171.
6. https://www.firstthings.com/article/2021/02/evangelicals-and
   -race-theory?fbclid=IwAR2EYdQNc2b4tqduO6T1NFTb0Ep
   CN7MOKfBs9hOTQzYRdHapnBsHXFKz5Ng.
7. Ibid.
8. https://www.blackenterprise.com/black-lives-matter-corporate
   -america-has-pledged-1-678-billion-so-far/.
9. St. Cyprian, *The Lapsed*, The Newman Press, 1956, p. 19.
10. Ibid., p. 27.
11. Ibid.
12. St. Cyprian, *The Lapsed*, p. 17.
13. 1 Corinthians 5:13 NIV.
14. Robin DiAngelo, *White Fragility*, Beacon Press, 2018, p. 1.
15. https://www.dailymail.co.uk/news/article-9749517/An-anti-racist
    -author-Robin-DiAngelo-makes-728K-year-speaking-engagements
    .html.
16. DiAngelo, *White Fragility*, p. 8.
17. Ibid., p. 10.
18. James 2:1 NIV.
19. Exodus 23:2-3 NIV.
20. Romans 3:23 NIV.
21. 1 Corinthians 10:13 NIV.
22. Ezekiel 18:20 NIV.
23. Deuteronomy 24:16 NIV.
24. Ephesians 4:18 NIV.
25. Colossians 2:13 NIV.
26. Ephesians 2:1 NIV.
27. Ibid.
28. Ibid.
29. Ibid.
30. 2 Corinthians 5:17 NIV.
31. Galatians 3:28 NIV.
32. Romans 6:18 NIV.
33. 1 John 1:6-10 NIV.
34. 2 Corinthians 6:14-16 NIV.

Chapter 5

1. http://www.hcs.harvard.edu/~gsascf/shield-and-veritas-history/.
2. George M. Marsden, *The Soul of the American University Revisited,* Oxford University Press, 1996.
3. Psalm 119:130.
4. https://www.thecrimson.com/article/2006/3/8/harvards -secularization-harvard-has-never-been/.
5. http://www.hcs.harvard.edu/~gsascf/shield-and-veritas-history/.
6. Romans 1:28 KJV.
7. https://www.nytimes.com/2021/08/26/us/harvard-chaplain-greg -epstein.html.
8. Marsden, *The Soul of the American University Revisited,* p.137.
9. For more on this, see the author's book, *The Christian Left: How Liberal Thought Has Hijacked the Church.*
10. Marsden, *The Soul of the American University Revisited,* p. 22.
11. Ibid., p. 90.
12. Ibid., p. 69.
13. https://news.harvard.edu/gazette/story/2016/07/in-long-hidden -bones-a-first-glimpse-of-philistine-lives/.
14. https://ui.adsabs.harvard.edu/abs/2003PhDT........33W/abstract.
15. https://www.dailybreeze.com/2008/05/16/art-stirs-debate/.
16. Ibid.
17. Ibid.
18. https://www.biola.edu/president/messages-media/contemplations -jesus-mural.
19. Ibid.
20. https://www.apu.edu/about/believe/.
21. https://www.theamericanconservative.com/dreher/hillsdale -college-azusa-pacific-black-lives-matter/.
22. https://pages.e2ma.net/pages/1767323/23410.
23. Dreher mentions that he adapts the professor's emails to help conceal his identity.
24. https://www.sgvtribune.com/2018/10/01/azusa-pacific-university -students-protest-after-reinstatement-of-lgbtq-relationship-ban/.
25. https://trackbill.com/bill/california-assembly-concurrent-resolution -99-civil-rights-lesbian-gay-bisexual-transgender-or-queer-people/ 1755865/.
26. https://www.bbc.com/news/education-55263392.
27. https://stream.org/new-california-bill-dangerous/.

28. https://www.washingtonexaminer.com/opinion/california-resolution -admonishes-anyone-who-doesnt-affirm-homosexuality-and -transgenderism.

29. https://www.crossway.org/articles/what-does-arsenokoitai-mean/.

30. Ibid.

31. Leviticus 18:22 NIV.

32. See also 1 Corinthians 9:6 and Jude 7.

33. Romans 1:26-27 NIV.

34. https://lawprofessors.typepad.com/nonprofit/2021/04/seattle -pacific-university-faculty-vote-no-confidence-in-board-over-lgbtq -exclusion.html.

35. The 45 Goals of Communism didn't appear in Skousen's book until the eighth edition in 1961; see *The Naked Communist*, Izzard Ink Publishing, 2017, p. 297.

36. Skousen, *The Naked Communist*, p. 307.

37. Ibid., p. 313.

38. Ibid., p. 308.

39. https://www.theblaze.com/news/2013/06/24/is-george-soros -secretly-funding-evangelicals-pro-immigration-reform-efforts.

40. Ibid.

41. Taken from a recording of a private conversation between the author and Michael O'Fallon at Liberty University on Saturday, November 14, 2021, at the Freedom Uncensored event.

42. https://www.bloomberg.com/news/articles/1993-08-22/the-man -who-moves-markets.

43. https://www.investopedia.com/terms/r/reflexivity.asp.

44. George Soros, *The Alchemy of Finance*, John Wiley & Sons, Inc., 2003, p. 374.

45. https://www.thegospelcoalition.org/article/indonesia-invitation/.

46. https://capstonereport.com/2020/10/23/reformed-theological -seminary-partners-with-convicted-clinton-donor-to-launch-center -for-reformed-theology/35095/.

47. https://www.biola.edu/president/leadership/board.

48. https://clarionproject.org/school-database/.

49. Ibid.

50. https://www.templeton.org/about/sir-john.

51. Ibid.

52. https://creationcare.org/what-we-do/an-evangelical-declaration-on -the-care-of-creation.html.

53. https://capitalresearch.org/article/creation-care-part-3/.
54. Ibid.
55. Ibid.
56. https://creationcare.org/what-we-do/an-evangelical-declaration-on
     -the-care-of-creation.html.
57. https://israelmyglory.org/article/the-money-behind-telos/.
58. Ibid.
59. https://www.jns.org/do-funders-like-george-soros-pose-a-threat-to
     -evangelical-christian-support-for-israel/.
60. https://www.camera.org/article/telos-group-promotes-anti-zionist
     -narrative-in-evangelical-community/.
61. Ibid.
62. https://www.christiancentury.org/article/2014-04/support-israel
     -waning-among-evangelicals.

Chapter 6

1. https://news.yahoo.com/church-failed-covid-19-pandemic
    -210703774.html.
2. http://disciplesallianceq.org/glad-news/new-mexico-pastor
    -supporting-equal-marriage/.
3. A slang term to describe the controversial COVID-19 vaccination.
4. https://www.hsph.harvard.edu/magazine/magazine_article/
    a-gift-unsolicited-unrestricted-and-unexpected.
5. https://threadreaderapp.com/thread/1420784407812653059.html.
6. https://hoptownchronicle.org/a-letter-to-the-church-love-your
    -neighbor-by-following-stay-at-home-order-and-practicing-social
    -distancing/.
7. Ibid.
8. www.prochoiceamerica.org/wp-content/uploads/2020/05/
    Roundup_-Pro-Life-Hypocrisy-on-COVID-19_5.15.20.pdf.
9. https://www.christianitytoday.com/better-samaritan/2021/november/
    evangelicals-picked-wrong-covid-debate-heres-one-we-should
    -.html.
10. https://www.thegospelcoalition.org/themelios/article/the-new
    -testament-and-the-state/.
11. Ibid.
12. Exodus 1.
13. Joshua 2.
14. 1 Kings 18.

15. 2 Kings 11.
16. Esther 1.
17. Daniel 1.
18. Daniel 3.
19. Daniel 6.
20. Matthew 2.
21. Mark 2.
22. Acts 4-5.
23. Acts 16.
24. John Calvin, *The Institutes of the Christian Religion*, IV, 20:32.
25. Ibid.
26. I first heard of Dr. Kuyper from my friend Dr. Owen Strachan. I'm indebted to Dr. Strachan's continuation of Kuyper's work on the subject of sphere sovereignty and its role in helping to shape this section of the book.
27. https://reformationaldl.files.wordpress.com/2019/07/spheresovereignty_english.pdf, p. 4.
28. See Acts 17:28.
29. https://reformationaldl.files.wordpress.com/2019/07/spheresovereignty_english.pdf.
30. Ibid
31. Ibid., p.16.
32. Ibid.
33. Ibid.
34. Ibid.
35. This does not preclude a believer's right to defend himself or herself.
36. 1 Corinthians 8:4-13 NIV.
37. In no way am I endorsing the use of the vaccine, but as a pastor, I won't also condemn someone for taking it. My focus is on the theology of the issue; there are others much more gifted than myself who can debate the ethical and scientific merit of the vaccine.
38. The same could also be applied to masks, forced quarantines, and other governmental controls.
39. 2 Corinthians 12:9-10 NIV.
40. https://www.theguardian.com/us-news/2021/sep/21/arkansas-black-community-vaccines-reverend.
41. https://abcnews.go.com/Politics/blessing-medicine-pastors-preach-covid-19-vaccination-gods/story?id=76367456.

42. https://kjzz.org/content/1547661/religious-leaders-urge-ducey -extend-stay-home-order.
43. https://www.ksdk.com/article/news/health/coronavirus/stl-faith -leaders-urge-people-to-stay-at-home-as-missouri-plans-to -reopen/63-35541702-1ba3-4901-8312-93f6f98527e2.
44. https://www.baltimoresun.com/news/bs-xpm-1997-05-29 -1997149029-story.html.
45. https://www.readex.com/blog/inherit-problem-how-lysenkoism -ruined-soviet-plant-genetics-and-perpetuated-famine-under.
46. https://www.crimemuseum.org/crime-library/international-crimes/ stalins-security-force/.
47. https://www.baltimoresun.com/news/bs-xpm-1997-05-29 -1997149029-story.html.
48. Ibid.
49. https://www.webmd.com/lung/covid-recovery-overview#1.

Chapter 7

1. https://www.detroitnews.com/story/news/nation/2018/06/18/ hillary-clinton-separating-families-border-moral-crisis/36151379/.
2. https://www.latimes.com/local/lanow/la-me-church-sanctuary -20180403-story.html.
3. https://twitter.com/aoc/status/1020105665166151683.
4. https://www.facebook.com/berniesanders/photos/it-is-an-absolute -moral-imperative-that-our-response-as-a-government-as-a-societ/ 2919648551423463/.
5. https://thehill.com/policy/energy-environment/580902-pelosi -defends-americas-moral-authority-on-climate-action.
6. https://twitter.com/hillaryclinton/status/612002144686874627.
7. https://www.startribune.com/rep-ilhan-omar-u-s-losing-our -moral-high-ground-on-immigration/558507862/.
8. https://www.dissentmagazine.org/wp-content/files_mf/1530301531 GeltmanSpring_1958.pdf.
9. Ibid.
10. Ibid.
11. *Geworfenheit* in German.
12. *Dasein* in German.
13. https://link.springer.com/article/10.1007/s40961-020-00189-4.
14. https://en.wikipedia.org/wiki/Competition_(biology).

15. https://www.dissentmagazine.org/wp-content/files_mf/1530301531
    GeltmanSpring_1958.pdf.
16. Those who reject critical theory.
17. https://www.thepress.net/opinion/letters_to_editor/the-moral
    -decline-of-the-united-states-of-america/article_11f31368-ca79
    -11e9-a06e-8f5a40144b94.html.
18. Hebrews 13:8 NIV.
19. Of course, we all still say, "Morality is in decline." Even I, as the
    author, am guilty of this. But it's important that we realize, when we
    say it, what we mean. That Christian morality has been swallowed
    up and set aside by the new morality of the Left.
20. Hebrews 6:5 NIV.
21. James 1:25 NIV.
22. See Psalm 18:19.
23. Romans 8:29.
24. G. K. Chesterton, *Heretics*, John Lane, 1905, p. 8.
25. A belief that moral truths are relative to the individuals, geography,
    and time of those who hold them.
26. https://www.vatican.va/content/francesco/en/speeches/2013/march/
    documents/papa-francesco_20130322_corpo-diplomatico.html.
27. https://www.washingtonpost.com/video/national/activists-take
    -abortion-pill-outside-supreme-court/2021/12/01/b1f62f5e-d949
    -4969-9239-ecfc83f1ad20_video.html.
28. https://interestingengineering.com/the-transhuman-revolution
    -what-is-it-and-how-we-can-prepare-for-its-arrival.
29. https://www.theatlantic.com/ideas/archive/2019/06/noa
    -pothoven-and-dutch-euthanasia-system/591262/.
30. https://www.heritage.org/gender/commentary/7-reasons-why
    -the-equality-act-anything.
31. https://www.aclu.org/other/whats-wrong-fetal-rights.
32. https://www.theguardian.com/us-news/2020/mar/31/florida
    -megachurch-pastor-arrested-for-breaching-covid-19-health-order.
33. https://www.dezeen.com/2017/10/26/saudi-arabia-first-country
    -grant-citizenship-robot-sophia-technology-artificial-intelligence
    -ai/.
34. https://www.cnn.com/2021/11/05/politics/fact-check-biden
    -garbage-compensation-family-separation/index.html.
35. C. S. Lewis, *Mere Christianity*, First Touchstone Edition, 1996,
    p. 79.

36. https://academic.oup.com/spp/advance-article-abstract/doi/10.1093/scipol/scab058/6366837?redirectedFrom=fulltext.
37. Ephesians 6:10-17 NIV.
38. Matthew 24.
39. 2 Thessalonians 2:9-12, 15 NIV.
40. John 8:31-32 NIV.
41. Deuteronomy 7:6 NIV.
42. Ephesians 4:18 NIV.
43. Colossians 1:21-23 NIV.
44. John 3:16-21 NIV.
45. 1 John 1:8-10 NIV.
46. G. K. Chesterton, *The Everlasting Man*, 2012, Introduction.
47. Lucas Miles, *The Christian Left*, Broadstreet Publishing, 2021, p. 127.
48. Isaiah 61:4 NIV.
49. Isaiah 61:7 NIV.
50. Available at LucasMiles.org.
51. For more on the problem of evil, see Lucas Miles previous book, *Good God: The One We Want to Believe in but Are Afraid to Embrace*, Worthy Publishing, 2016.
52. Job 1:1 NIV.
53. Job 40:8 NIV.
54. Dr. Jim Richards, *God's Wisdom for a Fair and Just World*, True Potential, 2020, p. 104–05.
55. Job 42:2-6 NIV.

Chapter 8

1. Joseph Boot, *The Mission of God*, Wilberforce Publications, 2016, p. 32.
2. https://www.huffpost.com/entry/evangelical-christianitys-big-turn-off_b_59b2b0f3e4b0bef3378cdf91.
3. https://religion.wisc.edu/2018/12/23/sectarianism-a-blindspot-in-society-and-religion-michelle-thomas/.
4. https://independenttribune.com/lifestyles/faith-and-values/column-white-christian-bigotry/article_c41120fc-dcd5-11ea-bb9a-8feca8b4d619.html.
5. https://time.com/3450525/atheists-arent-the-problem-christian-intolerance-is-the-problem/.

6. https://www.usatoday.com/story/news/nation/2021/07/27/tn
   -pastor-greg-locke-says-masks-arent-allowed-bible-church/
   5385007001/.
7. As the author, I do not personally know Pastor Locke, but I'm certain we have mutual friends. By no means is this an indictment of his ministry, but if we cannot call out errors on the Left and Right, then we've pledged allegiance to partisanship and not truth.
8. https://www.cnn.com/2019/06/14/us/tennessee-preacher-cop
   -lgbtq/index.html.
9. Boot, *The Mission of God*, p. 33.
10. Proverbs 20:10.
11. https://www.dailymail.co.uk/news/article-10272963/Dr-Fauci
    -called-COVID-Wuhan-strain-drawing-comparisons-Trumps
    -China-virus-comments.html.
12. https://www.heritage.org/progressivism/report/what-does-the-left
    -mean-social-justice.
13. Ibid.
14. Ibid.
15. https://www.heritage.org/civil-society/commentary/justice
    -inequality-and-the-poor.
16. Dr. Jim Richards, *God's Wisdom for a Fair and Just World*, True Potential Publishing, Inc., 2020, p. 12.
17. N. T. Wright, *Evil and the Justice of God*, IVP Books, 2006, p. 43.
18. Ibid., p. 105.
19. 1 Corinthians 2:2 NIV.
20. Wright, *Evil and the Justice of God*, p. 102.
21. Ephesians 2:8.
22. Romans 3:9 NIV.
23. Deuteronomy 32:4 NIV.
24. James 4:12 NIV.
25. Isaiah 33:22 NIV.
26. https://www.faithwire.com/2021/12/13/its-very-fake-female
    -upenn-swimmers-speak-out-over-trans-teammate/.
27. Hebrews 11:6 NIV.
28. Luke 18:1-8 NIV.
29. https://www.ashevillenc.gov/news/asheville-city-council-hears
    -next-steps-in-reparations-process/.
30. https://evanstonroundtable.com/2021/12/04/evanston-reparations
    -committee-grants-cpah/.

31. https://tulsaworld.com/news/local/govt-and-politics/preparations
    -underway-for-discussions-on-possible-reparations-tangible
    -amends-for-harm-caused-by-tulsa-race/article_7c59127c-6417
    -11ec-9e2b-0bfd7fbee67c.html
32. John 8:3-11 NIV.
33. Luke 19:8 NIV.
34. https://businessmirror.com.ph/2016/02/13/why-the-eucharist
    -promotes-social-justice/.
35. 1 Corinthians 11:24 NIV.
36. 2 Timothy 3:1-9 NIV.
37. 1 Corinthians 1:18 NIV.
38. St. Augustine, *City of God*, p. 552.

Chapter 9

1. Craig S. Keener, *The Historical Jesus of the Gospels*, p. 349.
2. Genesis 1:1 NIV.
3. Colossians 1:15-17 NIV.
4. John 8:58 NIV.
5. George Eldon Ladd, *A Theology of the New Testament*,
   WM. B. Eerdman's Publishing Co., 1974, p. 277.
6. Ibid.
7. Johannes Weiss, *Jesus' Proclamation of the Kingdom of God*, Fortress
   Press, 1971, p. 88.
8. Meaning the Jesus as described in the Gospel of John.
9. Ladd, *A Theology of the New Testament*, p. 278.
10. Philippians 2:6-8 NIV.
11. Philippians 2:7 HCSB.
12. Isaiah 53:2 NIV.
13. Hebrews 2:14-15 NIV.
14. Isaiah 53:3 NIV.
15. 1 Corinthians 2:7 NIV 1984.
16. 1 Corinthians 2:7 NIV.
17. 1 Corinthians 2:8 NIV.
18. Galatians 4:4 NIV.
19. Colossians 1:26-27 NIV.
20. https://www.thepublicdiscourse.com/author/roberta-green
    -ahmanson/.
21. https://progressivechristianity.org/resources/you-are-god-the-true
    -teachings-of-jesus/.

22. https://www.patheos.com/blogs/barrierbreaker/everyone-in-the
-world-is-christ-and-they-are-all-crucified/.

23. Acts 17:23 NIV.

24. Acts 17:34 NIV.

25. Christ the Victor.

26. Gustaf Aulén, *Christus Victor*, Wise Path Books, 2016, p. 12.

27. Saint Irenaeus of Lyons, *Against Heresies*, Ex Fontibus, 2010, p. 360.

28. Ibid., p. 378.

29. 1 Corinthians 15:21-22 NIV.

30. Romans 5:12 NIV.

31. Romans 5:14 NIV.

32. Romans 5:15-21 NIV.

33. Aulén, *Christus Victor*, pp. 33–34.

34. Ibid., pp. 41–42.

35. 1 Kings 19:9 NIV.

36. 1 Corinthians 10:13 NIV.

37. Hebrews 11:35b-40 NIV.

38. James 1:2 NIV.

39. Matthew 10:28 NIV.

40. Jürgen Moltmann, *The Way of Jesus Christ*, Fortress Press, 1993,
p. 174.

41. Philippians 2:7 NIV.

42. Matthew 27:46 NIV.

43. Moltmann, *The Way of Jesus Christ*, p. 174.

44. Hebrews 2:14-18 NIV.

45. Aulén, *Christus Victor*, p. 34.

46. Colossians 1:15-23 NIV.

47. Romans 10:8 NIV.

Chapter 10

1. John 10:10 NIV.

2. Joseph Boot, *The Mission of God*, Wilberforce Publications, 2016,
p. 64.

3. Saint Augustine, *The Trinity (De Trinitate)* Second Edition, New
City Press, 2012, p. 178.

4. Boot, *The Mission of God*, pp. 54–55.

5. Ibid., p. 55.

6. https://en.wikipedia.org/wiki/Mayflower_Compact#Text.

7. Ibid.

8. Boot, *The Mission of God*, p. 66.
9. David Barton, *Original Intent* (Wallbuilders.com).
10. Boot, *The Mission of God*, p. 66.
11. https://pubmed.ncbi.nlm.nih.gov/14509111/.
12. Boot, *The Mission of God*, p. 58.
13. Ibid., p. 48.
14. Ibid., p. 58.
15. Ibid., p. 523.
16. For more on this, see my previous work, *The Christian Left: How Liberal Thought Has Hijacked the Church.*
17. https://www.edweek.org/teaching-learning/biden-administration -cites-1619-project-as-inspiration-in-history-grant-proposal/ 2021/04.
18. https://www.theguardian.com/commentisfree/2019/sep/21/culture -american-apple-pie-week-in-patriarchy.
19. https://www.theatlantic.com/politics/archive/2015/07/tanehisi -coates-between-the-world-and-me/397619/.
20. James H. Cone, *A Black Theology of Liberation, Fortieth Anniversary Edition*, Orbis Books, 2020, p. 110.
21. Scott David Allen, *Why Social Justice Is Not Biblical Justice*, Credo House Publishers, 2020, p. 195.
22. Deuteronomy 8:10-19 NIV.
23. Deuteronomy 6:7 and 9 NIV.
24. Deuteronomy 6:20-25 NIV.
25. 1 Corinthians 4:7-13 NIV.
26. 2 Timothy 3:12 NIV.
27. List adapted from 2 Corinthians 11:23-28 NIV.
28. Philippians 3:7 NIV.
29. Philippians 3:10-14 NIV.
30. 1 Peter 4:1-6 NIV.
31. Ibid.
32. Matthew 6:5 NIV.
33. James 1:2 NIV.
34. See Matthew 5:39.
35. John 15:18 NIV.
36. https://chinaafricaproject.com/analysis/is-china-really-playing-the -long-game/.
37. W. Cleon Skousen, *The Naked Communist*, Izzard Ink Publishing Co., 2017, p. 298.

38. Ephesians 4:25-27 NIV.
39. For more on this, read *The Christian Left: How Liberal Thought Has Hijacked the Church*, by Lucas Miles.

Acknowledgments

As a pastor and outspoken voice for biblical Christianity, I've learned how valuable true friends are, and at times, how hard they are to come by. Fortunately, I've been blessed with no shortage of people in my corner to whom I am sincerely indebted for their counsel, service, and support. Topping this list is first and foremost, my wife, Krissy, who has always believed in me more than I have believed in myself. Your support is more than I deserve.

This book would not be in your hands if it was not for Humanix Books, the book division of Newsmax, a media company that cares about the values we share. I'd particularly like to thank Mary Glenn at Humanix Books for seeing the value of this book in the mainstream marketplace and for working tirelessly to help me bring it to you and the world.

I'd also like to thank Matthew Faraci and his team at Gideon 300. Thanks for being someone who tells me the truth and always works on my projects as if they are your own. I'm also grateful for several other key individuals that either inspired aspects of the book or played a role in directing me to certain source materials. On that list are Kevin McG, CJ, and Cooper, as well as several friends who always prefer to remain anonymous.

It would also be shortsighted to fail to acknowledge the contributions of previous publishers, most recently, Carlton Garborg, who provided support for prior works and encouraged me to engage this topic from the start.

Lastly, I'd like to thank my church family at Nfluence Church for continuing to allow me the opportunity to work out and refine these ideas from the pulpit, and for granting me the time and freedom to put thoughts to paper.

Index

as performance-based, 96
Pro-Palestinian sentiments in, 83
seeing everyone as Christ in, 147–148
suffering and, 175
Unitarianism, 69
view of Christ in, xiv–xv, 159
views of the Bible and, xii
(*See also* Christian Left)
progressivism:
alienation problem in, 117–119
compassion of the church and, 124
in culture, xiii, 77
dark money of, 77–80
human suffering and, 155
(*See also* Left)
Pro-Life movement, 85–88
protests, 72–76
pseudo-Christian organizations, 77
public health crises, 85–87 (*See also* COVID-19)
Puritans, 162–167

Q hypothesis, 28–30

race and racism, 35–50
Aryan Christianity, 41–43
Black Liberation Theology, 36–41, 48–50
Christian Nationalism and, 43–48
systemic racism, 3, 54, 60–62, 105
Walker-Barnes' prayer, 35–37
Woke Christianity, 48–50
(*See also* Critical Race Theory [CRT])
racial superiority, Critical Race Theory and, 52, 55
reason, religion of, xiv

recapitulation, theory of, 149–153
Reconciling Ministries Network, 45–46
reflexivity, 78–79, 86
Reimarus, Hermann Samuel, 19, 20–21
renewal of the world, 161–180
America as privileged and ill-informed, 169–173
applying *missio dei* in, 167–168
autonomy vs. theonomy, 165–167
battle for, 178–180
Christians' role in, 176–178
missio dei, 161–165
suffering for Christ, 173–176
resistance, 89–93
revelation, as key Gnostic idea, 12
revisionist history:
Critical Race Theory and, 53, 54
as goal of communists, 76–77
Riady, Henry, 79
Riady, James, 79, 80
Richards, Jim, 128
Rinedahl, Jéaux, 75
Rockefeller Brothers Fund, 80
Rogers, David Wilson, 85–86
Rome, persecution of Christians in, 57–60
Russell, Nicole, 73

sacred, viewing everything as, 106–108
salvation:
Kant on, xiv
Paul on, 16
Wright on, 131
same-sex marriage, 85–86
Sanders, Bernie, 104
SBC (Southern Baptist Convention), 3, 46